Conservatism

Key Concepts in Political Theory

Conservatism

Edmund Neill

polity

First published in 2021 by Polity Press

Polity Press
65 Bridge Street
Cambridge CB2 1UR, UK

Polity Press
101 Station Landing
Suite 300
Medford, MA 02155, USA

ISBN-13: 978-1-5095-2705-2
ISBN-13: 978-1-5095-2706-9 (pb)

A catalogue record for this book is available from the British Library.

Library of Congress Cataloging-in-Publication Data

Names: Neill, Edmund, author.
Title: Conservatism / Edmund Neill.
Description: Medford : Polity Press, 2021. | Series: Key concepts in
    political theory | Includes bibliographical references and index. |
    Summary: "The evolution of conservative political thought from the
    French Revolution to today explained"-- Provided by publisher.
Identifiers: LCCN 2021001801 (print) | LCCN 2021001802 (ebook) | ISBN
    9781509527052 (hardback) | ISBN 9781509527069 (paperback) | ISBN
    9781509527090 (epub)
Subjects: LCSH: Conservatism--History. | Conservatism--Philosophy.
Classification: LCC JC573 .N45 2021 (print) | LCC JC573 (ebook) | DDC
    320.52--dc23
LC record available at https://lccn.loc.gov/2021001801
LC ebook record available at https://lccn.loc.gov/2021001802

Typeset in 10.5 on 12pt Sabon
by Fakenham Prepress Solutions, Fakenham, Norfolk NR21 8NL
Printed and bound by CPI Group (UK) Ltd, Croydon, CR0 4YY

For further information on Polity, visit our website:
politybooks.com

Contents

Acknowledgements

I was warned by a number of people that writing a short book, particularly on a large topic, is much harder than it looks – and so it proved. However, I was fortunate to be sustained in the process by friends and colleagues throughout the process. I would like to take the opportunity here to thank three particularly influential teachers, who in their different ways I have found genuinely inspirational: Professor Janet Coleman, Professor Jose Harris and Professor Michael Freeden. All three of them possess minds that are not merely immensely learned, but genuinely intellectually original. Apart from them, I would like to thank the following for their advice, friendship, and intellectual acuity: Michael Bacon, Callum Barrell, Dean Blackburn, Chris Brooke, Sarah Churchwell, John Davis, Hannah Dawson, Blake Ewing, Stephen Farrall, Dev Gangjee, John Gibbins, Lawrence Goldman, Naomi Goulder, Stuart Jones, Paul Lewis, Suzannah Lipscomb, Catherine Marshall, David Mitchell, Terry Nardin, Kieron O'Hara, Noel O'Sullivan, David Owen, Estelle Paranque, Joanne Paul, Mike Peacey, Jaya Savige, Christoph Schuringa, Nikita Sud, Tim Waters, Kevin Williams and Brian Young. Particular thanks too must go to Iain Hampsher-Monk and Nicholas Cole who provided generous advice and guidance on the eighteenth century, though it must be stressed that any errors remaining are my responsibility alone.

My editor George Owers was very patient with my delays,

but more to the point was an assiduous and acute reader. He also deserves considerable thanks for picking three anonymous readers of the manuscript who were encouraging but also constructively critical, in exactly the way that anonymous readers should be. They have undoubtedly improved the book, and I would have taken up even more of their suggestions if the number of words available had been greater. They have certainly given me plenty of interesting food for thought for future projects, and I am very grateful to them.

Last but not least my mother Heather, my late father Edward and my brother Greg have always supported my intellectual endeavours, even when times were tough (as they can be in academia). However, this book certainly could not have been written without the help of my partner Stefan Demetriou, who provided the very desk it was written on, but also much other support besides. The least I can do is to dedicate it to him.

1
Defining Conservatism

This book seeks to define the concept of conservatism and to explore its nature in the context of Western Europe and America, primarily looking at Britain, France and the United States. At first sight, this might appear to be a relatively simple task. For unlike some of the vaguer, more contested concepts in political theory, such as nationalism, populism or fascism, conservatism appears to have a relatively fixed and stable meaning. In particular, theorists investigating conservatism have often argued that conservatives advocate four key political commitments. First, they have argued that conservatives favour the importance of 'natural' forms of authority, such as the monarchy, the church, the nation and the family to guarantee social stability – as opposed to artificially designed 'rationalist' ones, particularly those provided by government. Second, relatedly, they have maintained that conservatives advocate 'evolution' over 'revolution', preferring incremental change over producing solutions from scratch, even if existing institutions are far from ideal. Third, such theorists have claimed that conservatives often consider human nature to be imperfect and fallible, with the result that they hold human inequality to be beneficial, or at the very least inevitable. Finally, within these limits, they have argued that conservatives often stress the importance of private property and capitalism in promoting individual freedom.[1]

The Challenge of Defining Conservatism

In fact, however, as soon as one considers the concept of conservatism more closely, it throws up difficult definitional and conceptual challenges. For although some thinkers usually described as 'conservatives' have upheld the four commitments just described, others have not necessarily advocated all of them, or even, in some cases, any of them (Eatwell and O'Sullivan 1989: 47–61). First, although conservatives have often argued that traditional forms of authority are important, even those that have done so have not necessarily denied the importance of the state. Thus, Roger Scruton in *The Meaning of Conservatism* (1980), to take one modern example, was quite happy to stress the importance of governmental authority and the rule of law, as well as highlighting the vital role of traditional institutions like the family in ensuring social solidarity (Scruton 2001: 39–41). Still less, in any case, have conservatives agreed on *which* institutions play the most vital role in providing authority. To some in the nineteenth century, such as the influential French theorist Joseph de Maistre, the religious authority of the church was vital; for others in the same century, such as the English conservative W. H. Mallock, let alone in the twentieth, it was largely irrelevant (Maistre 1820: 213; Ford 1974: 319).

Second, although it is true that conservatives have often been cautious about initiating far-reaching changes, there have certainly been instances where they have sought to change society fairly radically. Thus Margaret Thatcher and Ronald Reagan's conservative administrations in the 1980s in Britain and the United States initiated major changes that fundamentally altered the relationship of individual, state and society, including significant reductions in direct taxation, the privatization of many government-owned industries, a reduction in the power of trade unions and an increase in home ownership (Hoover and Plant 2015). Third, although many conservatives have indeed generally rejected more substantive forms of equality, on the basis that such 'levelling' is neither natural nor desirable, they have nevertheless differed significantly between themselves over the degree to which they reject equality and accept traditional social hierarchies. Thus, even in the nineteenth century, various American conservatives, however much they rejected any notion of 'social justice', nevertheless took the idea of formal political equality guaranteed by the US constitution as sacrosanct; by contrast, some more radical conservative thinkers, such as Heinrich von Treitschke in Germany, argued much more explicitly against equal political participation on the basis that this contradicted man's natural inequality (Sumner 1963; Dorpalen 1957).

Finally, although conservatives have often been supportive of both private property and modern capitalism as guarantees of freedom, there have also been important exceptions and qualifications. Edmund Burke, arguably one of the earliest British conservatives, thought that the success of the free market relied on existing social norms, rather than the other way round, and this suspicion of the market persisted amongst certain kinds of British conservatives well into the twentieth century – the renowned poet and conservative cultural critic T. S. Eliot being one such example. Furthermore, some conservatives – like Scruton, for example – have stressed that private property rights should not be immune from all interference by the state if the general material welfare of the population at large is endangered (Burke 1968: 140, 146; Eliot 1939; Scruton 2001: 97–9).

Defining Conservatism: One Key Concept?

In view of such difficulties, clearly a different approach is necessary in order to define and explore conservatism successfully. One strategy pursued by some scholars is to try to isolate a particular concept that is especially fundamental to conservatism. Thus Peter Dorey, in his book *British Conservatism: The Politics and Philosophy of Inequality* (2011), sought to identify conservatism with a fundamental commitment to upholding inequality, while Noel O'Sullivan, in his 1976 study *Conservatism*, focused on the 'imperfection' of human nature – and hence a commitment to limited government – as a key to understanding conservative arguments (Dorey 2011; O'Sullivan 1976: 9–31). But although both these books are perceptive and insightful, they are in danger of ignoring or excluding types of conservatism (or facets of conservative arguments) that do not fit well with their approach. We have already noted that conservatives differ over the degree to which they uphold inequality, and even if it is reasonable to claim that most conservatives take a more negative view of human nature than most liberals and socialists, it seems implausible to argue that such a view is *always* the key to understanding their arguments, let alone that this necessarily implies a commitment to more limited government. Although they certainly agreed that human nature was imperfect, paternalist conservatives in post-war Britain, like Harold Macmillan, tended nevertheless to stress the positive good that government could do in preventing unemployment and boosting economic growth; likewise, late nineteenth-century French conservative nationalists, such as Maurice Barrès, certainly stressed the positive role the state could play, even if they did not have an entirely positive view of human nature (Green 2002: 171–4; Jennings 2011: 456). At best, therefore, such an 'exclusionary' approach can be useful if we are seeking to produce normative arguments in favour of a certain type of conservatism. But as a more analytic, descriptive approach, which aims to delineate the richness and complexity of the tradition of conservative thought, it leaves much to be desired.

Defining Conservatism: Historical Approaches

Samuel Huntington: 'dispositional' conservatism

What, in particular, these definitional failures reveal is that we need a method of understanding conservatism that is more sensitive to the way in which it has changed and developed, that pays attention to the fact that conservatism is a dynamic, historically variable phenomenon, rather than a static one that can be defined purely abstractly. One way of trying to do this is simply to identify conservatism with the impulse to uphold the status quo – in other words, with the desire to resist any attempt at (significant) change at all costs. So, rather than attempting to define conservatism by referring to a fixed list of objectives, this method instead identifies conservatism as a mode of thought simply with being reactive. This approach was famously advocated by Samuel Huntington in his article 'Conservatism as an Ideology', where he defined conservatism as 'that system of ideas employed to justify any established social order, no matter where or when it exists, against any fundamental challenge to its nature or being, no matter from what quarter' (Huntington 1957: 455). As such, Huntington argued, conservatism is not a doctrine that has essential attributes which are transmitted through time, and hence also does not have set of classic studies associated with it, which are then constantly subject to reinterpretation and reassessment (but also retention). The advantage of such a definition is that it avoids trying to identify conservatism with a fixed, unchanging set of attributes, hence going some way to respecting its mutable nature. But it also has two significant problems. In the first place, it seems deeply counterintuitive to label monolithic totalitarian states such as Soviet Russia as 'conservative', purely on the basis that their institutions failed to adapt and alter. Secondly, such a definition makes no allowance for those cases where thinkers and politicians that most scholars and contemporaries would label 'conservative' – such as those associated with the Thatcherite revival of conservatism in the 1980s – undertake fairly radical innovations (even if they do do it in pursuit of a past set of norms).[2] Despite its formal admission of the historically variable nature of conservatism, therefore, such a definition ultimately remains too formal to do justice to the way in which conservatism substantively develops, historically speaking.

In view of the difficulties involved with Huntington's definition of conservatism, other scholars – both from within the conservative tradition and from outside it – have sought to analyse conservatism in a more genuinely historical fashion, giving it a more substantive definition. Broadly speaking, there have been three ways of attempting this. First, some scholars have tried to define conservatism as being a nostalgic, backward-looking movement that seeks to uphold the institutions and practices of the pre-Enlightenment era. Conservatism then consists of trying to retain at least some of the pre-Enlightenment norms of religious belief, of monarchy and of hierarchy in society in general, against the corrosive modernizing forces associated with the Enlightenment in theory, and with the French and industrial revolutions in practice. On such a definition, a particular concern for conservatives is the attempt to uphold pre-modern forms of authority that were in danger of being undermined by Enlightenment rationalism – by its scepticism about religious belief, demands for equal representation, and rejection of aristocratic hierarchy, all of which had come to fruition during the French Revolution. Such pressures on traditional forms of authority, it is also maintained, have been heightened by some of the effects of modern capitalism, with its corrosive effect on traditional social and political hierarchies, so that a key concern of conservatism is to uphold the importance of a respected and beneficent aristocracy in order to maintain both order and social harmony (Kirk 2008; Vincent 2010: 57).

This definition of conservatism, however, has some significant weaknesses. It is useful in identifying certain tendencies within conservatism, particularly in the nineteenth century (as we shall see in Chapter 2), when a host of writers from Edmund Burke to Joseph de Maistre lamented the passing of the *ancien régime* and of pre-industrial social arrangements, at least to some extent. And its focus on the conservative criticism of Enlightenment rationalism highlights a tendency that remains important even in modern conservative thinkers who are less obviously nostalgic, notably John Gray.[3] But the trouble with the definition is that it significantly underplays conservatism's capacity for innovation. Even in the nineteenth century, some conservatives increasingly subscribed to certain 'Enlightenment' norms by embracing capitalism and representative government. And in a contemporary context, whatever reservations thinkers such as Gray have had about the philosophical justifications for modernity provided by the Enlightenment, they have nevertheless accepted most of its political programme, including the equal right to political representation, the stress on private property, and the fundamental importance of the concept of the 'rule of law'. Such a definition, then, clearly fails to capture the full meaning of conservatism.

Michael Oakeshott and Ian Gilmour: 'traditionalist' approaches to defining conservatism

Rather than trying to define conservatism as being largely backward-looking, therefore, other theorists, particularly within the conservative tradition itself, have sought to conceptualize conservatism as being an attempt to manage change cautiously. Such theorists include the British Conservative cabinet minister from the 1980s Ian Gilmour, and the influential mid-twentieth-century political philosopher Michael Oakeshott. Key to their analysis of conservatism is their claim that it does not simply consist of trying to uphold the status quo or of returning to a previous 'golden age'. Rather, they argue that conservatism is to be identified by its commitment to careful, organic, evolutionary change, contrasting this with more radical or progressive approaches, which are characterized as 'ideological' in the sense of being more self-conscious, more perfectionist, more radical and less respectful of tradition. Thus, Oakeshott famously suggested that a conservative's attitude to change is to be 'warm and positive in respect of enjoyment, and correspondingly cool and critical in respect of change and innovation', while Gilmour compared a conservative approach to change with that of an architectural conservationist who may regret the destruction of historic buildings, but nevertheless admits that a certain amount of updating and alteration is necessary (Oakeshott 1991: 412; Gilmour 1977: 122). To be a conservative, on such a definition, is to 'pursue the intimations' of the Western tradition, in Oakeshott's phrase, rather than trying to impose a new artificial pattern on it. This meant that conservatives could indeed extract from their political tradition certain kinds of ends that they ought to be pursuing – as opposed to lurching off in uncharted new directions like the rationalists, or trying to recreate some real or imagined past like more nostalgic conservatives. But at the core of this definition of conservatism was a particular conception of evolutionary change, with a bias towards preferring 'present laughter to utopian bliss', in Oakeshott's resonant phrase (Oakeshott 1991: 408).

To some extent, such an approach helps to reveal the nature of conservatism. It is certainly true that conservatives often tend to favour cautious, evolutionary change over radical innovation, seeking to uphold the worth of established institutions rather than setting up institutions from scratch. (For precisely this reason, Oakeshott himself was highly suspicious of the process of the establishing of the American constitution, despite its having some definite conservative aspects.[4]) Furthermore, perhaps more interestingly, how Gilmour and Oakeshott themselves sought to define the nature of tradition proves to be unconsciously revealing of how conservatives very commonly seek to conceptualize its nature. For by seeking to establish a sharp divide between a 'legitimate' approach to tradition, which respects its continuity and subtleties, and an 'illegitimate' one, which does violence to it by abruptly forcing it in a new direction, conservatives often set up a pronounced dichotomy between a 'natural' (or quasi-natural) approach to traditional norms on the one hand, and an 'artificial', 'ideological' one on the other.[5] This is clearly a strategy conservatives often employ, either explicitly or covertly, to try to render more progressive alternatives illegitimate.

However, there are also two problems with this definition. First, as we have seen, it is not always true that conservatives content themselves with the strategy of trying to ensure that historical change occurs in a cautious and evolutionary fashion. Rather, in some instances, conservatives themselves seek to initiate change, sometimes of a radical kind, with the aim of restoring a previous status quo. (For example, as noted earlier, an important component of the conservatism of the Thatcher and Reagan governments was their attempt to reverse developments they regarded as illegitimate, not least those associated with rises in direct taxation and the expansion of the welfare state.) Second, although the attempt by conservatives to present their approach to tradition as uniquely 'natural' or perceptive may well be revealing of their ideological strategy, it cannot be accepted as an objective analysis of conservatism. For whether or not conservatives are convincing in their particular interpretations of tradition and their responses to it, what they advocate cannot simply be assumed to be 'natural'; rather, as with all such responses to tradition, this is a claim that must be argued for.

Karl Mannheim: conservatism and traditionalism

This aspect of conservatism, stressing the extent to which it represents a particular response to changing social and political conditions – rather than simply doing one's best to 'follow' the norms that an authentic tradition bestows – is particularly highlighted by the third method of analysing conservatism historically. The most sophisticated version of such an approach was put forward by the influential early twentieth-century sociologist Karl Mannheim, in his book *Conservatism: A Contribution to the Sociology of Knowledge* (1925). For Mannheim, as for others seeking to analyse conservatism historically, conservatism must be distinguished from mere 'traditionalism' – in Huntington's sense of being purely 'reactive'. But, according to Mannheim, neither can it be identified with a purely backward-looking ideology, nor with the attempt to maintain and nourish a 'natural' ongoing tradition. Rather, he argues, conservatism must be regarded as a peculiarly *modern* response to sociological changes (ultimately initiated by the industrial revolution) which pose a challenge to traditional social structures and modes of political thinking. In particular, Mannheim argued, what originally inspired conservatism was a fourfold set of sociological changes associated with the modernization of society.

These are, first, the unification of societies, so that discrete, self-contained social units are joined together, often within the nation-state; second, that within such unified societies there develop differing social strata, some favouring progress, while others favour reaction; third, that divergent 'worlds of ideas' corresponding to these different strata also appear; and fourth, that these divergences increasingly take on an explicitly political character – so that the struggle between progressive ideas and those of reaction are increasingly fought out in an explicitly political sphere (Mannheim 1986: 83–6). All of these related developments mean that those seeking to preserve older social and political structures can no longer simply assume their worth and durability, but instead must explicitly argue for them. Hence the appearance, Mannheim argued, of a self-conscious conservatism,[6] which has two key features.

First, it is an explicit ideological position, which comes into being in response to dramatic social changes, in order to combat the progressive political ideologies associated with those changes. Conservatism, in other words, is itself a *modern* phenomenon, since, prior to the Enlightenment and the industrial revolution, it had no *raison d'être*. Second, as an explicit ideological position, conservatism seeks to put forward a comprehensive alternative to the core concepts of liberal Enlightenment thought, favouring above all an emphasis on the concrete over the abstract. So, Mannheim argues, rather than stressing universality, abstract natural rights and rationalism in general, as the Enlightenment thinker does, the conservative seeks to emphasize the importance of different individual situations, the holistic nature of society, and a dynamic, historical approach to reasoning – of 'history, life, and nation', as he puts it. As such, the Enlightenment concept of 'freedom', for example, is not simply rejected by the conservative; rather, it is recast as something concrete, historically specific and only comprehensible within a wider social framework (Mannheim 1986: 107–10).

In suggesting that conservatism is best defined as an explicitly modern phenomenon that specifically emerges to combat the effects of sociological changes and progressive ideologies associated with the French Revolution, Mannheim provided a more promising definition than those who seek to identify conservatism with a backward-looking nostalgia or an adherence to a single natural, hegemonic, tradition. Moreover, his observation that conservatives have often sought to rebut progressives' arguments by contending that their abstract concepts are better defined in concrete and historically situated terms provides a valuable insight into how conservatism operates. However, given Mannheim's focus on conservatism's origins, what his account lacks is a full account of how conservatism develops, and in particular of what provides it with lasting coherence as it has evolved and mutated from its beginnings in the late eighteenth century to the present.

Michael Freeden's Approach to Political Ideologies

To provide such an account, arguably the most convincing theoretical model is that advocated by the contemporary scholar Michael Freeden, most notably in his groundbreaking work *Ideologies and Political Theory* (1996). Freeden argues that although Mannheim's work is insightful, conservatism should not just be viewed as a peculiarly 'reactive' movement but as a full-scale political ideology. By this he does not mean to label conservatism as a delusion, a form of 'false consciousness' in the Marxian sense of the word, since on his definition an 'ideology' does not represent a limited, blinkered view of political life, incapable of adaptation. Rather, for Freeden, an ideology is a sophisticated and flexible way of understanding political life, which exhibits not only a certain degree of systematization of ideas, but also an ability to adapt, to respond to changing historical and political circumstances (Freeden 1996: 124–7). An ideology is, in other words, usually capable of mobilizing active political support as well as inspiring intellectual statements – and re-statements – of its ideas (Freeden 1996: 16, 552–3). As such, he argues, political ideologies are not crudely organized around one particular concept, but instead have a conceptually complex internal structure. While they will have some stable 'core' concepts, which remain fairly constant, they also have 'adjacent' and 'peripheral' concepts, whose relationship with each other and with the core changes over time, as their relative importance alters (Freeden 1996: 77–91). Indeed, in some cases, even concepts that have previously been at the core of an ideology may cease to be so, and become adjacent concepts instead (Freeden 1996: 84). Thus, Freeden argues, while liberals almost always set 'liberty' as a core concept at the heart of liberalism, precisely what liberty actually *means* will be affected by its changing relationship with adjacent and peripheral concepts within the ideology. For example, in mid-nineteenth-century liberal political theory in Britain 'liberty' was generally defined in contradistinction to 'society' and 'social welfare', but by the beginning of the twentieth century, in the work of such theorists as L. T. Hobhouse and J. A. Hobson, the idea that guaranteeing welfare was indispensable to the pursuit of liberty – and indeed that one of the main points of that pursuit was to ensure the flourishing of society in general – had become far more prevalent. 'Society' had thus become a concept adjacent to 'liberty' in liberal political theory; indeed, in some cases it had become more or less inseparable from it. Conversely, the right to individual private property, which for some liberal theorists had been a core component of liberalism and a key guarantor of freedom, became far less central, given the new stress on the flourishing of society at large (Freeden 1996: 202–9). Likewise, the demand for equal voting rights for women – a largely peripheral component of liberalism in nineteenth-century Britain – became by the early twentieth century increasingly linked to another of its core concepts, namely that of progress.

How, then, does Freeden think that conservatism functions as a political ideology, and what does he believe its 'core concepts' to be? Echoing some of the arguments we made earlier, he concedes that it is difficult to identify conservatism with a set of substantive core concepts in the same way that one can with the more 'progressive' ideologies of liberalism and socialism, since the ideological commitments of conservatives have been so variable. Rather, he seeks to build upon the more historically focused analyses of conservatism that we examined above, but to combine them into a more sophisticated structure. He argues that conservative ideology has four 'core' concepts – which of course can be combined with various (often more substantive) 'adjacent' and 'peripheral' ones. The core concepts are, first, a commitment to controlling or managing historical change, which at the very least favours caution in altering the status quo over radical change, and may (more ambitiously) claim that only change in accordance with 'natural' development or an 'organic tradition' should be considered legitimate. Freeden thus picks up Oakeshott's and Gilmour's arguments about conservatives following a 'natural' tradition, but treats these as a statement of conservative ideology, rather than as objective descriptions about tradition and historical change (Freeden 1996: 332–3).

Second, Freeden maintains that conservatives almost always contend that social and political institutions are shaped and constrained by 'extra-human' forces – forces independent of human control such as 'God', 'history', 'biology' or 'order', depending on the era. In other words, rather than viewing social and political institutions as being primarily created by conscious individual effort, conservatives argue – or indeed often *assume* – that the survival of these institutions depends on respecting such quasi-natural forces. Thus, in the nineteenth century, conservatives deemed it vital to the social order that there was a strong sense of hierarchy within society – sometimes buttressing such claims with evolutionary arguments about race – while in the twentieth century they often took economic arguments, whether Keynesian or post-Keynesian, as having an unquestionable, quasi-scientific status. And conservatives have almost always demanded that the family be accorded particular respect as a 'natural' institution. For Freeden, this explains the scepticism that conservatives usually exhibit about the possibility of improving social and political institutions by conscious design, since the stress on the vital nature of 'extra-human' factors in conservative thought demotes the importance of human agency and purpose, setting up a sharp dichotomy between the 'natural' evolution of institutions on the one hand, and the 'artificial' imposition of human design and planning on the other (Freeden 1996: 334–5).

These are conservatism's two most fundamental core concepts, according to Freeden. But they are also combined with two others that, together with conservatives' dislike of rapid and radical change, help to reveal why conservative beliefs have been so historically variable. First, going beyond Mannheim's important insight that conservatives develop their concepts about freedom, rationality and the social order in reaction to those of progressives, Freeden stresses that, for conservatives, such concepts never play an identical role in conservatism as they do in liberal or socialist ideology. Although Mannheim is entirely right to stress that conservative concepts are formulated as (more concrete) polar opposites to those of the progressives, Freeden argues that this misses an important and fundamental point about conservatism. For, rather than constituting the core of conservative ideology in opposition to progressive ideology, such concepts always remain to some extent adjacent to the *real* core concepts of conservatism – namely the desire to manage change, and the conviction that human actions are always subject to 'extra-human' influences.

This helps to explain the variability of such concepts within conservatism, Freeden argues, since on the face of it conservatives appear to be fundamentally inconsistent, variously advocating the importance of aristocratic hierarchy, mass democracy, income inequality and relatively generous welfare states. But in fact, these radical inconsistencies become readily explicable if they are viewed as subsidiary to the core conservative desires to control change and treat human agency as subject to an 'extra-human' order, since such *adjacent* conservative concepts are always constituted as responses to progressivism, just in divergent ways at different times (Freeden 1996: 335–40). Indeed, Freeden emphasizes, it is important to stress that conservatives' formulation of such concepts is far from being a passive process; rather, they are chosen precisely to combat whichever 'threat' to the current social and political order seems most pressing. (To give just one of Freeden's examples, in mid-nineteenth-century Britain, Victorian conservatives sought to combat liberal demands for more equal rights, particularly voting rights, by stressing the importance of a pre-existing aristocratic order for ensuring social and political stability; by the early twentieth century, however, they were instead stressing the virtues of universal private property rights against incipient demands for socialist redistribution [Freeden 1996: 339–40].) Paradoxically, Freeden argues, this can mean that if progressive demand for change is particularly strong, conservative support for the status quo can harden into conceptual rigidity, since although in the longer term a major strength of conservatism is its adaptability, in the shorter term the form conservatism takes is always parasitic on its progressive opponents (Freeden 1996: 341–2).[7]

One key factor, then, in understanding how conservatism operates and why it puts forward such an array of different positions, is that it has fundamentally different core concepts from those of the progressive ideologies. Thus, conservatism does not simply provide alternative definitions of such core progressive concepts as 'liberty', 'progress' and 'equality', but accords them a merely adjacent status within its ideological position. However, Freeden argues, conservatism's diversity and complexity can only truly be appreciated if we highlight a second factor in its response to such ideologies: not only does conservatism seek to formulate concepts in opposition to the most pressing threat to the social order, but it also often misinterprets (wilfully or otherwise) what the actual core concepts of such progressive ideologies are. Thus many post-war conservatives, confronted with the core socialist demands for greater equality and community, often chose to conceptualize such aims as being identical to the *adjacent* socialist demand for greater nationalization, with the result that conservatives appeared to be stressing privatization and decentralization as core concepts. Equally, a common conservative strategy to combat Marxism has been to conflate all forms of the ideology with 'totalitarianism', to imply that all Marxist movements are necessarily committed to state violence – a charge that is clearly fairer in some cases than others. And this phenomenon may be further complicated, Freeden argues, by the fact that conservatives sometimes decide they have previously been genuinely mistaken about the nature of their ideological opponent, with the result that they revisit their judgement about the nature of the threat, and pursue policies that appear to be aiming to put the clock back, rather than merely controlling or limiting social or political change. Thus many British and American conservatives in the 1980s clearly felt that they had been mistaken about the degree of state intervention they had allowed to occur since the end of the Second World War, with the result that they recalibrated their approach to give a greater prominence to individual liberty and private property within the conservative conceptual arsenal than had been the case in recent times. In such cases, the ideological position remains genuinely conservative, Freeden argues, since it is designed to preserve a pre-existing social order – just one that had existed rather earlier than the present. But the tactics involved then become, at least on the surface, rather more radical (Freeden 1996: 343–4).

What Freeden's analysis of conservative ideology allows us to do, then, is combine the more historically focused attempts at understanding conservatism we examined earlier into a more satisfactory structure. Rather than trying to analyse conservatism as purely backward-looking, or as an attempt to remain true to a particular tradition, or even simply as a sophisticated reaction to progressive ideologies, Freeden incorporates all of these into a method of analysing conservatism as a fully fledged ideology, based around the core concepts of managing change and of an 'extra-human' dimension to individual agency. What this helps to explain above all is how flexible and adaptable conservatism is. For although, as Freeden argues, all sophisticated political ideologies have the ability to evolve and adapt, this ability is especially central to conservatism – even if it comes at the cost of being parasitic on more progressive ideologies – since, according to his account, conservatism arises directly in response to progressive attempts at amelioration and alteration.

One major advantage of such an approach is that it removes the need to distinguish the various different types of conservatism radically from one another, redefining them in terms of other conceptual vocabulary, whether this be as varieties of the political 'Right' – such as 'moderate Right', 'radical Right', 'extreme Right' – or in terms of other vocabulary altogether, such as 'Christian democrat', 'romantic' or 'reactionary'. This of course does not preclude making distinctions between different types of conservatism. There are, for example, important differences of emphasis between those forms of conservatism that tend to favour a more active attempt to return politics and society to an earlier point; those that are pessimistic about the current prospects for successful adaptation without the survival of earlier norms, but see little prospect of retaining or resuscitating them; and those that are more cautiously optimistic. One may even contend that Freeden should have made more of these differences of emphasis in his analysis. But this should not detract from his major achievement in establishing that all such ideological positions are ultimately species of *conservatism*, rather than being radically separate forms of right-wing thinking.[8] What Freeden's approach provides, in other words, is a way of identifying what differentiates conservatism from other ideological positions while also respecting its extreme adaptability.

However, what Freeden in *Ideologies and Political Theory* does not give us is a full account of how conservatism has evolved historically as a political ideology. This is entirely understandable in a pioneering work that seeks to prove the importance of a whole new area of scholarly study, but such an account is nevertheless vital, given conservatism's intrinsic variability. While conceptual analyses of the different forms of conservatism are essential, particularly in view of the myriad forms the ideology can take, nevertheless, given that the very essence of conservatism is to be oppositional, to seek to control change, we need to trace its evolution historically in order to understand it properly. Such an approach has two advantages in particular. First, it enables us to explore the development of conservatism in the context of its struggle with rival ideologies, examining how it has sought to combat various progressive threats from liberalism and socialism (amongst others) during its long and complex history. Second, it also enables us to chart how conservatism is to be distinguished from political ideologies and movements which, although distinct, have at various points been closer to conservatism than the more progressive ideologies. Thus, at various historical junctures, movements such as 'libertarianism', 'nationalism', 'Christian democracy', 'populism' and even 'fascism', to name only the most influential, have been deemed to overlap with conservatism. Analysing conservatism in a historical and developmental fashion enables us to examine the degree to which such movements have been similar to conservatism, and even in some cases provided intellectual ammunition for it.

Plan for the Book

Where, then, should our investigation of conservatism start? This innocent-sounding question in fact conceals a keenly fought debate about the origins of political ideologies, including liberalism and socialism as well as conservatism. For even if we exclude other countries and focus solely on Britain, there is considerable disagreement about when one can start talking of 'conservatism' and 'liberalism', as opposed to older labels and dichotomies like 'Court' and 'Country' or 'Tory' and 'Whig'. Thus Robert Eccleshall, for example, introducing a well-known anthology of English conservatism, begins his survey of conservative thought with Charles II's Restoration in 1660, but eschews using the term 'conservatism' until he reaches the eighteenth century (Eccleshall 1990). Other more recent commentators have suggested that it is a mistake to apply the label to any period before the beginning of a more 'professional' politics at the end of the nineteenth century, or even genuine mass democracy in the twentieth (Bourke 2018). Moreover, such disagreements only proliferate if we expand our focus to encompass other countries and regions, since industrialization, the 1848 revolutions in Europe, slavery, imperialism and mass politics, for example, have had differing effects on different countries at different times.

Nevertheless, there seems good reason to begin our survey of conservatism in the late eighteenth century, which commentators have long viewed as a plausible place to seek the birth of modern political ideologies, in view of the triple effects of the industrial revolution, the Enlightenment and the French Revolution. In particular, Mannheim's argument that there was no need for 'conservatism' as an ideology while previous early modern traditions went unquestioned remains a strong one (Mannheim 1986; Koselleck 2004). Given the limitations of a fairly short book, I will be confining my exploration of conservative development largely to Britain, France and the United States, with the occasional glance at Germany and Italy. Obviously to some extent such a choice is somewhat arbitrary, but, on the positive side, it still allows us to draw some important comparisons between how conservatives reacted to similar challenges in countries with very different national traditions, and to explore how Freeden's excellent analysis of conservatism can be applied in a wide range of different contexts.[9] Thus Chapter 2 seeks to examine how conservatives in Britain, France and the United States reacted to the French Revolution, industrialization and the Enlightenment, looking at the wide variety of responses in each country in turn.[10] Chapter 3 shifts to exploring how conservatives reacted to the 1848 revolutions, the intensification of nationalism and imperialism, and the advent of mass politics, taking the story up to the First World War. Chapter 4 then examines how conservatives responded to the development of mass politics, the advent of socialism, and mid-twentieth-century scepticism about political theory, amongst other challenges, from roughly 1918 to the 1960s. Finally, Chapter 5 explores how conservatives reacted to the end of the economic 'golden age' that followed the Second World War, the impact of the liberalizing movements of the 1960s, and the problems that New Right conservatism itself presented to more traditionalist conservatives. Finally, a brief epilogue cautions against predicting the demise of conservatism too readily.

2

Conservatism from the French Revolution to 1848

The Challenge of the Enlightenment, Industrialization and the French Revolution

This chapter will examine how conservatism developed from the advent of the French Revolution in 1789 to the 1848 revolutions in Europe and the American Civil War. Essentially, as we argued in Chapter 1, conservatism came into existence in this period as a reaction to the industrial revolution, the Enlightenment and the French Revolution. Because they posed such an overt challenge to previously existing traditions, these three phenomena inspired an explicit ideological reaction – in the form of conservative ideology. However, delineating precisely how conservatism developed in these years is a complicated task, for three reasons.

First, the industrial revolution, the Enlightenment and the French Revolution were all complex, multi-stranded, even occasionally contradictory phenomena, and hence diagnosing the challenge they posed to conservatives is not simple. The industrial revolution, for instance, had an impact not only on the nature of work and production and the relationship between agriculture and industry, but also on the development of banking and credit, since the latter proved essential to a developing industrial economy (Lee 2006: 46–7). And in view of the urbanization that industrialization caused, it also raised questions about how such newly urbanized areas should be represented politically and their social problems dealt with – whether by the state or through other agencies.

Equally, the 'Enlightenment' was a deeply complex and ambivalent intellectual movement, whose proponents differed amongst themselves, both philosophically and politically. Philosophically, under the influence of new seventeenth-century scientific methods, most notably those of Isaac Newton, Enlightenment thinkers tended to agree that the natural world could only be understood in terms of material processes, rejecting earlier Aristotelian doctrines that it should be viewed as purposive, in terms of a teleology.[1] But they differed significantly over the degree to which such methods could be used to explain human conduct, with some thinkers (such as the French physician and philosopher Julian Offray de La Mettrie) arguing that human actions could be understood purely in terms of material laws – if they could be understood at all – whilst others, notably Jean-Jacques Rousseau and Immanuel Kant, claimed that human agency was distinguished from natural processes by being the product of a free will (La Mettrie 1996; Rousseau 1923: 184; Kant 1997: A534/B562). Critically, too, they also differed over the degree to which human conduct could be understood as motivated by reason. For those amongst the Enlightenment thinkers who were 'rationalists', such as Kant, it was entirely plausible to claim that human behaviour could be understood as (ultimately) the product of reason (Kant 1997: A651/B679). By contrast, for those like David Hume, who believed that reason could perform at best a calculative, instrumental function, it made much more sense to view human conduct as ultimately motivated by 'passions' – by desires and traditions (Hume 1965: 414–16). Politically as well, Enlightenment thinkers differed over what would guarantee an enlightened society, with some, such as Voltaire, favouring the regimes of 'enlightened despots' such as Frederick the Great, and others, such as Jeremy Bentham in his later work, arguing that only a fully democratic state could eliminate corruption and maximize the happiness of all (Bentham 1973: 295–6).

Finally, although in one sense the French Revolution was clearly an epoch-making event, one which for many scholars marks the beginning of modernity, it too went through several different ideological stages, and hence had several conflicting political implications. Clearly it posed a challenge, in the most concrete sense, to the traditional institutions of the *ancien régime*, especially the Bourbon monarchy and the established church – and by extension to similar monarchies and churches across Europe. But whether the ultimate implication of the revolution was a moderate representative democracy (as recommended by the Girondins), a direct democracy backed up by a theory of universal natural rights (as recommended by the Jacobins), or the modernizing imperialism of Napoleon, was far less clear. That the revolution could inspire radical thinkers as different as Tom Paine, Richard Price and Thomas Jefferson is a testament to how diverse its political implications were.[2]

The second reason why it is difficult to identify how conservatives formulated their responses to the industrial revolution, the Enlightenment and the French Revolution is that conservative thinkers did not formulate their responses to these new developments purely reactively, in the sense of simply trying to reverse what had occurred. Given how complex and radical the changes involved were, this would have been a tall order in any case, but in fact early nineteenth-century conservatives, in harmony with the theory we put forward in Chapter 1, focused instead on trying to manage the pace of change, concentrating their fire on whichever innovations they felt were particularly harmful. Thus, for some conservatives, the most worrying modern development was the rise of modern commerce, which tended to dissolve the 'organic' relationships of pre-capitalist society by transforming all social relationships into those of property owner and labourer, or producer and consumer. For other conservatives, it was the rise of the rationalistic strain within the Enlightenment, with its tendency to undermine religious faith, that was most concerning. And for others again, it was the potentially destabilizing implications of the French Revolution, and especially its doctrines of natural rights and participatory democracy that were most worrying. To state this is not, of course, to suggest that there was no coherence to these responses or overlap between them – on the contrary, many, perhaps most, conservatives in this era were intent on upholding traditional structures of authority, religious faith, economic inequality and the importance of landed property. Rather it is simply to highlight what we saw in the last chapter – that although such ideological commitments are relatively stable (within the era we are considering), they ultimately constitute adjacent rather than core concepts within conservatism, so we should not expect to see conservatives espousing them in every case.

Finally, the task of delineating the nature of conservatism in the early nineteenth century is complicated still further by the obvious fact that particular national and political circumstances often had a significant role in determining both the threats to the pre-existing order and the resultant conservative response. If there were some significant similarities between conservative positions in different countries in this period, nevertheless the national background against which conservatives operated also clearly played an important role. Thus, in Britain, a common conservative response to the effects of the French Revolution and an increasingly industrial society was to emphasize the importance of preserving traditional intervening institutions between individual and state, and to restate the importance of tradition and the common law. Conversely, in France, although unsurprisingly conservatives were particularly preoccupied with combatting the effects of the revolution, they were often less keen to stress the importance of traditional institutions in view of the widespread dissatisfaction with the *ancien régime*. And of course in America matters were different again, since however conservative some of the doctrines of the framers of the Constitution and of the *Federalist Papers* were – and, in a different way, those seeking to uphold traditional ways of life in the south – there was no escaping the fact that the republic was founded *de novo*, as an experiment, and that this coloured the doctrines of conservative ideological responses. To explore how conservatism developed in the late eighteenth and early nineteenth centuries, then, we will examine its development in different national contexts, firstly in Britain, before passing on to consider France, and lastly the very different world of the early republic in America.

Conservatism in Late Eighteenth- and Early Nineteenth-Century Britain

In late eighteenth-century Britain, even before the advent of the French Revolution, conservatism was evolving in a context where increasing commercialization and urbanization had already led to significant concerns about how society was developing. First, the advent of a much more commercially organised society had led to concerns amongst some politicians and political thinkers as to whether this would adversely affect public morals.[3] Second, more concretely, the rising population, and in particular the spiralling costs of having to pay poor relief, raised genuine questions about the feasibility of feeding the British population, worries most pungently articulated in T. R. Malthus's *Essay on Population* (1798). Finally, the experience of fighting the American War of Independence, the notorious levying of 'taxation without representation', and the increasing urbanization in Britain itself had already sharpened worries about a political system that disenfranchised considerable numbers of even propertied voters.[4] Nevertheless, the advent of the French Revolution, and its subsequent effects on British politics, exacerbated such tensions considerably. During the Revolutionary War itself, the genuine threat of invasion, and the stimulation of radical ideologies in Britain, sometimes supported by the theory of universal natural rights, constituted the most immediate threat to the status quo. After the war, the considerable increase in public debt and the resultant tax rises also significantly increased socio-economic tensions within society, particularly after the revolutionary and Napoleonic wars finally ended in 1815. Moreover, the incorporation of Ireland into the United Kingdom in 1801, with its huge number of Catholic citizens, helped to raise even more sharply the question of reforming the electoral franchise. For if Catholic troops could be relied upon to fight against Napoleon, when the British state was at its greatest peril, what reasonable justification could there be for continuing to restrict the vote to Anglican citizens alone?

Edmund Burke

In this challenging context, British conservatism evolved in three distinct ways to try to control social and political change. The first was that of one of the most influential conservative theorists of all, Edmund Burke, whose conservatism was primarily inspired and provoked by the French Revolution itself. Burke had been a moderate reformer before the revolution, a cautious sympathizer with the grievances of the American colonists, an advocate of reforming British imperial institutions (notably the East India Company), and by no means the most doctrinaire upholder of Anglican privileges against Catholics and Dissenters. But he was violently affected by the experience of the French Revolution, and in response, put forward a series of arguments in his *Reflections on the War in France* (1790) that can clearly be regarded as conservative, even if Burke himself never used the term.[5] For although it is true that the *Reflections* were certainly not written as a sober and analytic work of political theory, but rather as a contribution to a fierce contemporary debate about the implications of the French Revolution, nevertheless a careful reading of the work reveals a relatively systematic conservative position, organized around the ideology's core concepts of controlling historical change, and the importance of influences beyond human agency. In particular, Burke's arguments were based upon a commitment to the concept of tradition, which performs two major functions in his thought.

First, a crucial part of Burke's argument was to insist that tradition, and the concepts he associated with it, namely 'custom', 'habit' and 'prejudice', are superior motivators of human conduct compared to abstract reason. In other words, in contrast to the arguments of the more rationalist Enlightenment thinkers, such as Richard Price and Tom Paine, and particularly those of French revolutionaries, Burke argued that it is much better for individuals to rely on such learned tendencies as custom and prejudice – as opposed to abstract reason – because doing so 'does not leave a man hesitating in the moment of decision, sceptical, puzzled, and unresolved' (Burke 1889: III, 81). By contrast, if humans attempt to rely on their reasoning abilities alone, they run the risk of having to agonize over their decisions – partly because they have to consider, self-consciously, each and every problem, but also because, by ignoring custom and prejudice, they reject all the inherited communal resources that tradition bequeaths, throwing them back upon their individual calculative ability. Thus, Burke argued, even irrational prejudices are superior to abstract, self-conscious reason, since they motivate us regularly and reliably in a way that reason cannot. Hence Burke's position was fully in keeping with one of the fundamentals of conservative ideology in that he strongly emphasized the importance of an extra-human factor (namely tradition) for the successful performance of human conduct; individual decision-making alone is not sufficient.

Second, however, it is important to note that in drawing a contrast between 'tradition' and 'individual reason' in this way, Burke was defining these concepts in a very particular manner that favours a conservative political ideology. It is true that by arguing that reason is not a particularly good motivator of human conduct, as compared to habit or prejudice, Burke was merely following a significant number of other prominent eighteenth-century thinkers (including both Hume and Rousseau). But by explicitly linking this argument to upholding the importance of tradition, he was making a much more distinctive claim: the concept of 'tradition' in Burke's account becomes the repository of the wisdom of generations, a set of customs and institutions that have gradually developed, naturally and organically, in a way that continues to offer us a vital guide to future action, and which cannot be replicated by the conscious application of individual abstract reason. As Burke himself put it, appealing to tradition in this way is beneficial because it 'furnishes a sure principle of conservation, and a sure principle of transmission; without at all excluding a principle of improvement' (Burke 1968: 120). Hence, although we are dependent on the gradually acquired experience of previous eras, this does not preclude the possibility of progress, through cautious evolution or trial and error. Indeed, Burke went even further and argued that relying on tradition is not merely *sensible*, but also *natural* – because, he claimed, 'we receive, we hold, we transmit our government and our privileges, in the same way we enjoy and transmit our property and our lives', by which he means family inheritance (Burke, 1968: 120). By contrast, if we abandon 'the general bank and capital of nations and ages' provided by tradition, then we are left at the mercy of our individual reasoning abilities, where ultimately the only underlying motive for action is self-interest, and the only method of ensuring order is explicit, overwhelming power (Burke 1968: 183).

These definitions explicitly ruled out the possibility that abstract reason alone could help us form stable, authoritative governments, and indeed also severely limited the possibility that reason could help us interrogate our tradition without irreparably damaging the benefits of its inheritance. By limiting the critical power of abstract reason in this way, thereby significantly insulating British cultural and political norms from criticism, Burke performed the classic conservative move of redefining a core progressive concept – in this case, reasoned progress – so as to oppose it with a more seductive conservative alternative. Moreover, by claiming that the power of reason is limited, and conversely that the power of tradition should be respected, Burke also provided a justification for the conservative argument that cautious, incremental change should be preferred to radical transformation. A particular conception of history and tradition thus played a key role in Burke's thought.

What, more substantively then, did Burke think must be conserved from our tradition, so that we can maintain and develop our social and political institutions and face the future with confidence? Essentially, he argued there are five achievements in particular that must be retained and built upon, sharply contrasting the organic, incremental change practised in Britain with the attempts by the revolutionary French to remake their political institutions anew, using the power of abstract reason alone. First, he stressed the value of the common law, which in many ways epitomized Burke's emphasis on the importance of incremental change. For in stressing the value of precedent in developing case law, as opposed to consciously designed legislation, Burke underlined his commitment to cautious evolutionary change, to trial and error, in opposition to the attempts of the French revolutionaries to produce an entirely new system of laws. This of course did not rule out the possibility of gradual improvement, but any progress had to be based upon a reverence for the legal inheritance we have been bequeathed, on the realization that such an inheritance cannot be consciously replicated.[6]

Second, in parallel with this argument, but more fundamentally, Burke argued that the state itself should be regarded as complex and organic, benignly bequeathed to us by a beneficent tradition, rather than as an artificial construction that can be consciously designed by pure reason. Part of his rationale for arguing in this way was obviously to oppose the French revolutionaries' attempts at constructing a state entirely anew, through reason alone. But Burke also wanted to repudiate any attempt at conceptualizing the state as a contract, as an entity whose legitimacy fundamentally depends on the continuing consent of its participants, as John Locke in particular had famously argued.[7] Instead, Burke argued, the state should be seen as a sacred trust, as part of a constitutional inheritance entailed to the current generation, and of which they are only 'life renters' (Burke 1968: 192). As such, their relationship to the state cannot be one of a contract; rather they have a duty to maintain, nourish and obey the state, so that they can pass it in a healthy condition to future generations – the relationship is fundamentally one of duty, not a contractual one.[8]

For Burke, then, the state must be conceptualized as part of the constitutional inheritance we have been bequeathed. However, it is important to stress that, for Burke, the state only represented *part* of that tradition, that constitutional inheritance. It is, he argues, precisely one of the most nightmarish aspects of the French Revolution that it sought to abolish all intervening institutions between individual and state, reducing men and women to one undifferentiated mass of individuals. For the relationship of the individual and the state to be a truly healthy one, we also need to retain and nourish three other aspects of our tradition.

Thus the third aspect that Burke believes must be conserved from tradition is the wide set of relationships that we now refer to as 'civil society', which, he maintained, connects individuals together through habit and affection, rather than cold hard reason. These local attachments include everything from the family and our neighbourhoods to our local pubs and regional justices. Burke famously referred to these as 'little platoons', and argued strongly that 'to love the little platoon we belong to in society is the first and necessary step that leads us to patriotism' (Burke 1968: 135). Without such traditional and habitual affections, in other words, individuals would not develop a genuine loyalty to the state, and it is precisely the tragedy of the French revolutionaries that they abolished the traditional local attachments that bound individuals together, thereby inevitably undermining such loyalty.

Fourth, continuing the theme of promoting loyalty to the state and preserving crucial elements of tradition, Burke also stressed the vital role of religion. In arguing that religious belief was necessary to induce people to behave morally, since it provided both hope of everlasting life and fear of utter damnation, Burke was hardly an unusual thinker in the eighteenth century. Even as radical a thinker as Rousseau had wrestled with the problem of how to ensure that individuals in modernity acted morally under the social contract, agonizing over whether a 'civil religion' alone was sufficient for the purpose (Rousseau 1923: 121–2). But Burke went further than this, arguing not merely that religious belief is necessary for people to behave morally, but also that it formed an essential part of their traditional inheritance, which helped them to have proper reverence for the state. This was important for the subjects governed by the state, in order to guide them away from falsely conceptualizing their relationship with it as a contract, hence ensuring proper stability (Burke 1968: 191). But it was equally important for those in office, since traditional religion helped to fill those exercising authority with an appropriate degree of awe in the face of their responsibilities, hence ensuring good governance and the continuity of the state (Burke 1968: 189). In order for Christianity to perform this role of sanctifying the political order, Burke maintained, an established church was necessary, and one with considerable temporal resources. For not merely must the church be able to influence the state through its rich cultural tradition and impressive heritage of accumulated learning, it also needs sufficient property to be independent of the state, to be rich and powerful enough to command awe and exert direct influence (Burke 1968: 272, 203). As such, Burke argued, the church needs to own sufficient land for this to be possible, and any attempt at expropriating its land for immediate gain, or to service government debt, is liable to end in disaster. This point leads to the final element of tradition that Burke felt it vital to conserve – landed property. Rather than allowing land to be bought and sold like any other commodity, Burke thought it vital that the traditional structure of land ownership should to some extent be preserved, in order to maintain social order and (as we have just seen) traditional cultural structures through the aristocracy and the church. This did not mean that Burke was necessarily opposed to the market or the increase in commercial activity that was such a feature of late eighteenth-century British society. Indeed, he argued that 'moneyed' activity, entrepreneurial activity, was not just tolerable but *necessary*, since it is 'enterprising' and innovative – as opposed to traditional landed agricultural activity, which was 'sluggish, inert and timid'. This was because Burke thought it crucial that states evolve, rather than just preserve their previous features. As he put it, 'a state without the means of some change is without the means of its conservation' (Burke 1968: 140, 146). It was in fact precisely one of the problems of the French *ancien régime* that it had been too stratified, according to Burke, elevating a landed aristocracy over the entrepreneurs to too great an extent, thus stifling innovation and creating deep social resentment of a kind not found in Britain. But despite all this, it was still crucial to insulate land from market pressures, since otherwise aristocratic values such as honour and chivalry, which were inextricably linked to the maintenance of landed property, would be undermined – with the ironic result that the continuing viability of the market itself would be endangered (see Pocock 1982). Only by retaining such aristocratic values could the stability necessary for trade within the market be maintained, Burke argued; by contrast, market processes themselves, by rendering all commodities (including land) exchangeable and 'volatilized', tended to cause instability.[9] For the ultimate nightmare for Burke was the situation that had occurred in France, where land (and particularly church land) had been particularly debased, since it could be purchased by paper money, in the form of the new *assignats*. Since this currency was sustained solely by provisional subjective opinions, by speculation, it put land on an even less stable footing than it would be if purchased by more conventional money (Burke 1968: 310–11). Even worse, Burke argued, given that the *assignats* were liable to decrease in value, the situation was likely to degenerate further. For having expropriated church lands in the hope of reducing its national debt, the French state would find that purchasers of this land would pay for it in increasingly worthless *assignats*, with the result that it was all too likely to resort to further expropriation in the hope of improving its situation. In other words, Burke argued, as soon as land becomes reduced to the level of other assets, the danger of destabilizing society and subverting tradition becomes all too real.

In response to the French Revolution, therefore, Burke produced a highly coherent set of conservative arguments in favour of cautious evolutionary change. Nevertheless, despite the power of those arguments, the ending of the Napoleonic wars in Britain presented new problems for conservatives, since progressive demands that could be ignored during the wars – notably to reduce wartime debts, crack down on government sinecures and corruption, remove religious barriers for Catholics and Dissenters, and reform the voting system – were now thrust to the forefront of the agenda. Broadly speaking, conservatives adopted two strategies to deal with these problems, both with mixed success.

Post-1815 conservatism: 'liberal Toryism'

First, one influential group of conservatives often known as 'liberal Tories', many of whom were supporters of the government of Lord Liverpool (1812–27), sought to address many of these progressive complaints directly, arguing in favour of reducing government corruption and debt, and, in harmony with this, of administrative reform in order to re-establish the authority of the state. Thus proponents of liberal Toryism, such as William Huskisson, Lord Castelreagh, Sir Robert Peel and above all George Canning, argued for reducing sinecures, curtailing the practice of bribing MPs to vote, and overhauling debt repayment procedures to improve government finances. To reinforce this, they also argued in favour of improving the government's administrative and legal processes, through radical reform of customs legislation, obtaining much better statistical information from both local authorities and the colonies, and rationalizing the criminal law (in particular the reduction of capital offences) (Parry 1993: 34–8). Crucially, however, liberal Tories differed from progressive liberals in advocating greater freedom in the market, not simply in order to increase efficiency, or because they thought it would automatically improve individuals' characters, but because they considered the market itself to be a moral testing ground, where good and bad conduct was rewarded or punished. (Unsurprisingly, perhaps, such beliefs often harmonized well with various forms of evangelical Christianity.) So, even though liberal Tories clearly differed from Burke in being keener advocates of increased market freedom, they remained decidedly 'conservative' rather than 'liberal'. The difference was simply that, in contrast to Burke, they emphatically conceptualized the market itself as one of the 'extra-human' constraints on human conduct, rather than giving it the ambiguous status he did (Hilton 1988: 221).

Furthermore, underlining their conservatism, and in contrast to a number of their radical opponents, liberal Tories flatly refused to countenance any extension of the voting franchise, arguing that increasing the number of voters would not necessarily represent public opinion any better. Instead, they felt, it would inevitably undermine respect for property rights and superior intelligence (Parry 1993: 45–9). For, liberal Tories argued, the representation of 'public opinion' always meant in practice representing a diversity of different political interests, and there was no guarantee that extending the franchise would represent these interests better. Meanwhile, the danger, as in the French Revolution, was that 'superior intelligence and superior property would be overborne ... [in favour of] the very worst and vilest species of despotism – the despotism of demagogues', as Peel himself put it (Hansard HC Deb., 19/22 April 1831).[10] Despite some concessions to liberalizing the workings of the market and reforming the inefficient parts of government and the legal system, 'liberal Tories' thus remained, at heart, emphatically conservative.

Post-1815 conservatism: 'romantic Toryism'

If liberal Tories sought to address progressive demands after the Napoleonic wars by reducing corruption in government, improving legal and governmental efficiency, and embracing the possibilities offered by the market, the response of the second group, perhaps best described as 'romantic Tories', was very different. For these conservatives, who included literary figures such as Robert Southey, William Wordsworth and Samuel Taylor Coleridge, the liberal Tories' approach was deeply inadequate, since they believed it was the market itself that lay at the root of many of the problems that had emerged in the early nineteenth century.[11] Attempting to meet progressive complaints about government corruption and increasing poverty with a response that continued to uphold the importance of the market was thus deeply problematic, since doing so ignored the fundamental cause of many modern social problems. Far from being an arena that encouraged moral behaviour, so the romantic Tories argued, the market, and the newly emerging theory of 'political economy' behind it (as put forward variously by Adam Smith, Malthus and David Ricardo), was having deeply damaging effects on the very fabric of British society.[12] This was because the market undermined the traditional habits and reciprocal obligations that had previously existed between different classes, and reduced all relationships to the achievement of short-term gain. The result of the increasing scope of this 'commercial spirit', to use Coleridge's phrase, was inevitably that individuals were encouraged to think of themselves in terms of crude materialistic economic classes, and hence to demand the vote along these lines. This, Coleridge argued, would only further undermine a historic constitutional settlement which had recognized and represented a complex hierarchy of interlocking local, economic and professional interests, organized organically (Coleridge 1969: IV, 128).

As such, romantic Tories sought ways to tame the commercialism of the market and re-establish proper social and political obligations between classes. To some extent they differed between themselves over precisely what would accomplish this best. Thus Coleridge stressed the necessity of combating modern materialism by re-moralizing the landed gentry through a rediscovery of the truths of seventeenth-century Christian Platonism, which he proposed to do by empowering a 'clerisy' within the Church of England to provide intellectual and moral guidance – though he did not think this necessarily precluded Catholic emancipation or the repeal of the Test Acts, provided that the prestige of the Anglican Church was not threatened. Wordsworth, by contrast, was suspicious of such speculative philosophy, however well intentioned, and preferred to rely instead on people's spontaneous feelings, particularly the charitable impulse to provide relief for the poor, though he too sought to uphold the values of the landed gentry and the British constitution. And if Southey, for his part, was more implacably opposed to the removal of religious restrictions for non-Anglicans, he was if anything even more keen than Coleridge to combat the effects of modern industrialization through state action – including redistribution through taxation, factory regulation and the education of all citizens (Morrow 2011: 41–51; Eastwood 1989: 327–31). But all of these romantic Tories, in their different ways, sought to diffuse the negative effects of the modern market, managing change by looking to the past to ameliorate its impact.

Conservatism in Late Eighteenth- and Early Nineteenth-Century France: The Revolution and Its Aftermath

As in Britain, conservatism in France in the late eighteenth and early nineteenth centuries appeared in response to a combination of three challenges to traditional authority. These were first the challenge of rationalist Enlightenment thinkers, the *philosophes*, such as Denis Diderot and the Marquis de Condorcet, to the legitimacy of the institutions of the *ancien régime*; second, that of sceptics and anti-clericalists to the established church; and third, that of constitutional innovators seeking to challenge the traditional role of the aristocracy and secure wider representation for the people, partly in response to an increasing population. However, there were also three important (and related) differences in the way these challenges manifested themselves in the French context, with the result that the forms conservatism took were significantly different to those in Britain.

First, French conservatives were confronted even more directly with the reality of the Revolution itself, which presented them with a number of difficulties. Most obviously, despite the popularity of Burke's *Reflections* in France (where it was rapidly translated after the revolution) (Draus 1989: 79), the option of a Burkean conception of conservatism, upholding an unbroken tradition of beneficent habits and institutions, was not available, given the radical and far-reaching effects of the revolution.[13] But the revolution also presented other challenges. In particular, given that it evolved from being a declaration of the fundamental rights of man in 1789, to the infamous and bloody Terror of 1793 under Robespierre, to a full-scale imperialist enterprise under Napoleon Bonaparte in the early nineteenth century, the question of which parts of France's chaotic political tradition ought to be maintained to manage historical change most effectively became a highly complex one. Second, on a related point, while few conservatives, even the most reactionary ones, thought it possible to revert to the political arrangements of the *ancien régime*, nevertheless a choice had to be made as to which aspects of it were most crucial to retaining a continuing social order. Thus, for some, the maintenance of the Catholic Church was of crucial importance; for others this was not the case. Finally, while British conservatives certainly objected to aspects of the Enlightenment, for their French counterparts the question of how fully to reject the Enlightenment and which of its innovations were most pernicious was more stark. This was because French conservatives had a much more immediate stake in judging the degree to which Enlightenment thought itself was responsible for the outbreak of the revolution, or even the Terror. And this in turn led many of them to fixate upon the extent to which Rousseau's conception of the state in particular – with its radical dismissal of traditional institutions, its insistence that sovereignty always remained inalienably with the people, and its alleged underlying individualism – was an important factor in the breakdown of the old order (Jennings 2011: 112–20).

Arguably, this led to the advocacy of three main types of conservatism in late eighteenth- and early nineteenth-century France, spanning the 1789 Revolution, the 1814 Restoration of the Bourbon monarchy and the establishment of the July monarchy in 1830.

Moderate reform: Jacques Mallet du Pan

First, one version of French conservatism responded to the challenges of the eighteenth century and the revolution by advocating moderate reform of the *ancien régime* (and later a return to a reformed version of it). While these conservatives sought to retain the monarchy and uphold property rights, and were generally sceptical of the worth of abstract principles, they nevertheless tended to be critical of some of the excesses of the *ancien régime* and sceptical of the privileges of the Catholic Church. An important example of this type of conservatism is the work of Jacques Mallet du Pan, a Genevan theorist and journalist, who ultimately ended up in exile in Britain. His works included the *Considérations sur le Gouvernement de France* (1764) and *Considérations sur la Nature de la Révolution de France* (1793), and he edited the *Mercure de France* from 1783.

To some extent, despite the differences in context, Mallet du Pan put forward arguments that are comparable to Burke's version of conservatism. Like Burke, he rejected the possibility of basing of political arguments on purely abstract principles, arguing that such a mode of argument is based upon a desire for certainty, and underlying this a 'confusion of ideas, an anarchy of opinion [and] a universal scepticism' (Acomb 1973: 68–9). Furthermore, like Burke, Mallet du Pan's suspicion of trying to replace an understanding of human passions and knowledge of history with abstract principles only increased as he watched the French Revolution unfold, exasperatedly declaring that 'it is absurd to talk ceaselessly of principles, where one only finds circumstances' (Mallet du Pan 1793: 77). And again like Burke, Mallet du Pan, even at his most liberal, was determined to reject any suggestion that sovereignty within a state ultimately resided in the people – in sharp contrast to the arguments put forward by Rousseau in *The Social Contract*. (Thus even when arguing in his first work, the *Compte Rendu* [1770], that the children of non-citizens in Geneva, the *natifs*, should be given greater political recognition, Mallet du Pan rejected such a doctrine.)

However, there are also four significant differences between the two theorists, which highlight Mallet du Pan's greater moderation. First, unlike Burke, Mallet du Pan emphatically rejected the proposition that the revolution itself could be blamed upon Enlightenment rationalists, upon the *philosophes*, arguing that while 'the badly regulated spirit of philosophic disorders' may well make revolutions worse, what causes a revolution is ultimately a political event, the displacement of power (Godechot 1971: 78). (This also marked him out from many French counter-revolutionary critics, who very specifically blamed Rousseau for the outbreak of the revolution.) Second, on a related point, although as adamant as Burke that the 1789 Declaration of the Rights of Man was a mistake, Mallet du Pan, unlike Burke, opposed it primarily on the pragmatic grounds of its vagueness and impracticality, rather than because any reliance on written constitutions was necessarily a mistake. Since abstract doctrines and declarations only have force if accorded the backing of positive law, the appropriate method of assessing new constitutions and declarations, Mallet du Pan argued, was to work out how effectively they can be put into practice. If one applies this test to the Declaration, he argued, the conclusion must be that its highly generalized principles, in view of their sweeping nature, will be useless if not applied, and deeply dangerous if put into practice (Godechot 1971: 74).

Third, partly because of his closeness to the reality of the *ancien régime*, Mallet du Pan was far less willing than Burke to mount an argument based upon the continuity of tradition, and he continued to argue for reform of the constitution after 1789 – unlike Burke who rapidly recoiled from the outbreak of revolution. Although the political solutions Mallet du Pan put forward were ones that Burke would largely have approved of[14] – namely a constitutional monarchy with bicameral representation, with one of the houses analogous to the House of Lords – unlike Burke he was not inclined to sympathize overmuch with the fallen monarchy. In particular,

Mallet du Pain partially blamed the *ancien régime* for its own demise, by yielding in the face of rioters, in a manner sharply different from Burke (Godechot 1971: 75). Finally, although keen to uphold the importance of property rights, and even willing to countenance a continuing role for the aristocracy after the revolution, Mallet du Pan was arguably more overtly critical of feudalism than Burke, and certainly less worried about the expropriation of church property. It is true that he remained as convinced as Burke that a maintenance of religious belief was necessary for societies to remain moral, and he was thus just as hostile as Burke to the idea of the church being undermined entirely. Nevertheless, he was far less convinced of the damage of removing the Catholic Church's traditional privileges and landed property (Godechot 1971: 75).

'Theocratic conservatives': Joseph de Maistre and Louis de Bonald

In short, therefore, if Mallet du Pan was deeply critical of the violence used to prosecute the revolution, and intent on upholding property rights, his version of conservatism was ultimately a relatively moderate one, which declined to reject all aspects of the revolution entirely. By contrast, other conservatives, such as the notorious Savoy writer Joseph de Maistre, and the Provençal nobleman Louis de Bonald, perhaps best labelled 'theocratic conservatives', objected much more strongly in the late eighteenth and early nineteenth centuries to the progress of the French Revolution, and in particular to its assaults on the Catholic Church. Although both of these thinkers were originally reformers – with Maistre seeking to strengthen the *parlements* as a way of restraining the Bourbon monarchy before 1789, and Bonald even initially welcoming the revolution as a way of revitalizing local government – nevertheless both were violently repulsed by the attacks on the monarchy and the Catholic Church as the revolution unfolded (Darcel 1988: 179; Klinck 1996: 25–34). In response, they vigorously reaffirmed the vital importance of religion and authority for a healthy political system. It is true that neither thought it was possible to return fully to the days of the *ancien régime*, with Maistre in particular famously declaring that one could as soon reverse the revolution as bottle the entire contents of Lake Geneva. Nonetheless, both theorists mounted a full-scale denunciation not only of the revolution itself, but also of what they saw of its intellectual causes, in the hope of reforming the French political system. In particular, in their most famous works – Maistre's *Considérations sur la France* (1797) and *Du Pape* (1819) and Bonald's *Théorie du Pouvoir Politique* (1796) – both theorists argued that the fundamental cause of the Enlightenment, and ultimately of the revolution, was the Protestant Reformation. Both agreed that the Reformation had encouraged destructive individualism, since Protestantism – 'the son of pride, the father of anarchy, the universal dissolvent', as Maistre put it in typically lurid terms – directly encouraged men to trust their own opinions, rather than having these guided by authority, tradition and above all by established (Catholic) religious truths (Lebrun 1965: 138). More than this, however, Maistre and Bonald argued that the individualist scepticism enabled by the Reformation led to three damaging developments, which (they claimed) underpinned the Enlightenment and ultimately led to the French Revolution.

First, both theorists, and Maistre especially, took issue with the epistemological scepticism they took to be representative of the Enlightenment as a whole, attacking Locke's empiricism in particular for arguing that mankind could adequately understand the world through a combination of simple ideas acquired from experience and the mental reflection that combines such ideas. Such arguments, Maistre insisted, did not really explain how the process of mental reflection that generated more complex 'general' ideas worked, and hence he concluded that Locke was wrong to dismiss the proposition that mankind depended on innate, pre-experiential, God-given ideas to understand the world (Jennings 2011: 328). Second, both theorists were deeply sceptical of the contention – which they saw as invented by Francis Bacon, but popularized by the Enlightenment – that empirical scientific investigation provided the only certain knowledge about the world. Not only did this ignore the fact that without innate ideas we would be unable to understand the world at all; more seriously it threatened to undermine

religion by making God utterly inaccessible to human understanding (Maistre 1998: 14). Finally, Maistre and Bonald
argued that the Enlightenment, by popularizing the idea that
mankind should be conceptualized as a set of individuals
divorced from God, opened the way to Rousseau's dubious
and destructive political theory, with its insistence that
men in the state of nature were naturally solitary, and that
therefore in order to form an authoritative government,
individuals had to choose it voluntarily, through a form of
'social contract' whereby individual 'wills' were to be harmonized in a General Will.

Such thinking explained, all too clearly, Maistre and
Bonald thought, where the initial ideas for the revolution
came from – but these ideas were fatally flawed, and for
two reasons. First, there was little evidence to suggest, as
Rousseau had claimed, that men had originally been solitary
and noble; rather, Maistre and Bonald both insisted, it
was much more likely that they had always been naturally
social and were damaged by original sin (Maistre 1884: VII,
563). Second, on a related point, both claimed that because
Rousseau's theory of the social contract was fundamentally
individualist, his attempt to formulate a 'general will' was
necessarily doomed to fail, since it implied an integration of
many individual 'wills' in a way that was simply not possible.
(As Bonald put it, Rousseau's conception of the general will
implied that 'the will of a people in their entirety, even if it
is unanimous ... is only the sum of its particular wills', so
that ultimately these individual wills remained different and
separate [Jennings 2011: 119].) Hence, both argued, it was
no wonder that using such a theory to found a new republic
was bound to end in disaster, since aiming at a chimerical
'general will' would inevitably lead to the republic dissolving
and disintegrating into individuals and factions, rather than
truly aiming at the general good.

What solutions did Maistre and Bonald propose in response
to these problems they identified with the revolution and the
Enlightenment? To some extent they agreed with Burke's
argument that a critical problem with both the revolution
and the Enlightenment was that they ignored the importance of the wisdom bequeathed by tradition, attempting to
replace it with abstract, *a priori* principles in a way that was

doomed to failure. Thus Maistre and Bonald's complaint that the Enlightenment thinkers, and the advocates of the French Revolution, were always talking in the abstract about 'man', as opposed to people's natural, traditional identities as Englishmen or Frenchmen, members of families, or children of God, was one that Burke would very much have agreed with. But Maistre and Bonald also proposed three additional solutions, which marked them out as being significantly more radical.

First, they were more definite than Burke in rejecting the Enlightenment as a whole, and one of their key solutions to the problems it had brought about was to restore the power of the Catholic Church, and specifically of the papacy, in order to ensure political order (Maistre 1820: 213). Second, although Maistre and Bonald conceded that, since different nations had different cultures and political traditions, it followed that different political systems were appropriate for different countries, they nevertheless had a clear preference for a monarchy invested with 'sacred' power. The first genuinely stable political regime, Egypt, had been a monarchy, as opposed to the alternative models of Asiatic despotism and Roman empire, both of which had been unstable (Bonald 1859: I, 34). By contrast, the British model of monarchy, recommended by Burke and Mallet du Pan, was deeply inferior, because its powers were limited by parliament, because it allowed female rulers – who necessarily lacked authority – and above all because it followed a false version of Christianity, namely Protestantism (Bonald 1859: I, 77–8). Finally, Maistre and Bonald were more radical than both Burke and Mallet du Pan in that their method of understanding history, and of managing change, ultimately relied upon providence – it was a theodicy. However horrific the French Revolution had been, it was ultimately to be conceived as a necessary punishment from God, a way of combatting the evils of mankind and purifying the church, as Maistre in particular argued strongly (Maistre 1980: 34, 39). If this argument, and more generally Maistre's stress on the paradigmatic role of the executioner in ensuring order in every society, appears at first sight lurid, even fascistic, then what should be emphasized is how vital Maistre and Bonald considered the indivisible exercise of power to be for a well-ordered society (Berlin 1994: xxviii). The only way to conserve tradition properly was by (re-)establishing a monarchy with undivided power, backed by the guidance of true, Catholic, Christianity in the person of the pope. The revolution had shown, all too clearly, that half-hearted alternatives were insufficient.

If the 'theocratic conservatives' Maistre and Bonald produced a trenchant response to the revolution, and an aggressive critique of the *philosophes*, nevertheless their radical position was controversial, even amongst royalists and counter-revolutionaries and even during the revolutionary period itself. After the exile and final fall of Napoleon in 1814–15, working out how to respond to a rapidly changing set of circumstances before the founding of the Second Empire in 1852 – including the Restoration of the Bourbons, the July Monarchy of 1830 and the Second Republic in 1848 – proved challenging for conservatives, as indeed it did for other, more liberal political thinkers. Thus, in particular, deciding what the powers of the king, legislature and local government should be under a reformed monarchy, the extent to which Catholicism was necessary for a stable government, what could be learned from the *philosophes* and even the revolution, and whether ancient virtue was possible in an increasingly commercial society, all remained divisive questions.[15] Some conservatives, commonly referred to as the 'Ultras', such as the Comte de Montlosier in his *De la Monarchie Française* (1814), while not as extreme as Maistre and Bonald, nevertheless did everything they could to strengthen the powers of the monarchy in the 1820s and 1830s, though their efforts were set back by the final expulsion of the Bourbons in 1830. But many conservatives sought to negotiate the politics of the period more moderately, coming to terms with the founding text of the Restoration, the 1814 *Charte*, which combined rhetoric asserting continuity with the *ancien régime* with an acceptance of some liberalization – particularly freedom of worship, equality before the law and greater freedom of the press (Rosanvallon 1994). If they were not as fixated on liberty as were genuine liberals – such as François Guizot and the group he was associated with, the *Doctrinaires* – nevertheless they advocated a much more constitutional monarchy compared to the 'Ultras'. One key example of this moderate conservatism was the Vicomte de Chateaubriand.

Post-1815 conservatism: Vicomte de Chateaubriand

For Chateaubriand, there was no doubt that the French Revolution had been a cataclysmic event, but, unlike Maistre and Bonald, he did not characterize it as unique, but rather as a particularly dramatic example of a process that had been occurring since the time of the ancient Greeks. As such, in his *Essai Historique, Politique, et Moral sur les Révolutions*, published in 1815, Chateaubriand argued that although the *philosophes* were to some extent to blame for the revolution, by their corrosive questioning of established institutions and traditional beliefs, their writings could not be considered the real cause of it (Chateaubriand 1861: I, 548 n. 2). Rather, the revolution had been more or less inevitable, given that the advancement of civilization almost necessarily brought with it increasing wealth and corruption. Moreover, this tendency had been accentuated in France by the highly stratified court, where a weak king had been easily misled by 'incapable and wicked ministers' and their 'host of half-starved servants, lackeys, flatterers, actors and mistresses' (Chateaubriand 1861: I, 364). To some extent, therefore, Chateaubriand's argument read very much like a traditional republican critique of the dangers of wealth and civilization, but, just like Constant (and unlike Rousseau), Chateaubriand had already come to the conclusion that the project of establishing a virtuous republic in modern France (as the Jacobins had sought to do) was doomed to failure, not least because of the sheer size of the modern state (Jennings 2011: 245). However, given his keen-eyed critique of the *ancien régime*, by the time the Restoration occurred Chateaubriand was equally unconvinced that a powerful absolutist monarchy was the answer to France's problems in 1814.

Instead, Chateaubriand accepted the principles established by the *Charte*, but also sought to give them a distinctively conservative interpretation. Thus, unlike Maistre and Bonald, he agreed that a restored monarchy should have checks and balances, like the British version, with clear distinctions between the functions of the monarch and his ministers, and a bicameral parliament representing peers and commons. Moreover, he was also liberal enough to stress that ministers, and not the monarch, should propose legislation, partly because this protected the monarch, but also because it protected the liberty of citizens. However, Chateaubriand, like Burke, also stressed the vital importance of aristocratic norms for the continuing health of the restored monarchy, citing honour, loyalty and scorn of wealth for its own sake as values that were essential. In other words, if the revolutionaries had been justified in some of their material demands, their attempts at reforming morals completely had been much more destructive (Scott 2015: 169–74). After the publication of *Le Génie du Christianisme* in 1802, Chateaubriand also stressed the beneficial effects of Catholicism in sustaining a stable reformed monarchy, arguing that, far from being linked to savagery, darkness and slavery, as Voltaire and other *philosophes* had infamously claimed, Christianity in general, and Catholicism in particular, was responsible for most of what was most inspiring and sublime in Western civilization. Amongst others, these achievements included sculpture, drama, sacred music and painting (Chateaubriand 1966: I, 57). Moreover, Chateaubriand argued, the example of Britain proved that the clergy could safely be granted extensive property in a representative system, rebutting the revolutionaries' argument that this would inevitably lead to overwhelming corruption (Scott 2015: 173–4). In short, if Chateaubriand broadly accepted the principles of the *Charte*, his elaboration of how its principles should operate in practice exhibited a distinctively conservative lean, stressing the vital role of both church and aristocracy, and deprecating rapid revolutionary change.

Conservatism in the Early United States: Puritanism and Slavery

Turning to the United States, at first sight seeking to understand the nature of conservatism in late eighteenth- and early nineteenth-century America seems to be a distinctly unpromising idea. For, unlike Britain and France, the thirteen colonies, and the early United States, were not affected in the same way by the main factors that had caused conservatism to develop in Europe. First, although their intellectual lineage was undoubtedly complicated, many of the founding fathers of the United States, such as Thomas Jefferson, James Madison and Alexander Hamilton, had at least as much in common with British and European radicals as with conservatives, using the thought of the Enlightenment as inspiration for innovation and progressive causes, rather than reacting against it. The most obvious and extreme example of this is the major influence on American political thought of Thomas Paine, who famously argued in favour of the universal reasoning abilities of mankind, and that monarchies were inherently corrupt, in such texts as *Common Sense* (1776) and *The Rights of Man* (1791). However, he was far from being alone, other important Enlightenment influences on the founding fathers being Bacon, Newton and, above all, Locke. Bacon provided an inspiring model for how to undertake the empirical work necessary to found a new state; Newtonian laws were often claimed to be an inspiration for the perfection of the constitution (once established); while Locke's insistence that individuals only owed loyalty to the state insofar as it guaranteed their property rights provided both a justification for rejecting British authority and an influential model for governance in the early United States (Pole 1981: 195–6). Such a contractual model of the state, with its insistence that society should be conceptualized as a set of individuals, rather than organically, and that therefore tradition is relatively unimportant, was, of course, precisely one of Burke's main targets in arguing for his brand of conservatism.

Second, the reaction to the French Revolution was generally less hostile in the United States than in Britain, partly in view of the military assistance that pre-revolutionary France had given to the American colonists, negotiated by Benjamin Franklin, and because of the considerable (if not universal) antipathy towards Britain that continued to exist among Americans in the later eighteenth century. Certainly, there were fears about the more radical aspects of the revolution, and Congress even passed the Alien and Sedition Acts in the 1790s, with the aim of discouraging the immigration of revolutionaries from France. But reservations about some aspects of the revolution did not prevent the election of the pro-French Jefferson in 1800, nor a general sympathy for the ideals of the revolution, even if Americans generally disapproved of some of its excesses in practice (Samuelson 2003: 114, 125; Young 2011: 384–5).

Finally, the colonists and early inhabitants of the United States of the late eighteenth and early nineteenth centuries tended, on the whole, to be less perturbed by the advent of the commercial market than conservative thinkers in Britain and France. Whatever continuities with the past existed, the colonists were essentially establishing a new system of property ownership, so American political thinkers of the period tended to be sceptical that tradition alone could provide the system with legitimacy, preferring to see this as provided by individual effort and the workings of the market. Hence the popularity amongst many of Locke's theory that the legitimacy of owning property was intrinsically linked to 'mixing one's labour' with it. It is true that there certainly *was* ambiguity as to what exactly 'freedom' meant, both in theory and practice, with some (such as Jefferson) linking it much more closely with the ownership of land (often in the West), and others (such as Hamilton) linking it more directly to the ability to trade and labour freely within the market. Nevertheless, few sought to define freedom as Burke had done, linking it directly to tradition and distinguishing as sharply as Burke had done between land and other types of property (Young 2011: 384).

Where, then, should one seek to find conservatism in the United States in the late eighteenth and early nineteenth centuries? Initially, one should briefly note that four of the early arguments used to justify separation from Britain, advocate ratification of the constitution, and indeed legitimize the very constitution itself, arguably all had some conservative aspects. First, at least in the run-up to the revolution of 1776, revolutionaries often justified their position by arguing that either George III or the British parliament (or both) had violated the historic rights that the colonists had enjoyed as British citizens (Young 2018: 49). Second, the *Federalist Papers* (written jointly by Hamilton, Madison and John Jay) advocated the ratification of the new constitution partially on the basis that its checks and balances were necessary because human beings lacked sufficient virtue to sustain the new state without them. Rather than being full-scale advocates of liberal freedom, in other words, or of the possibility of republican virtue, the *Federalist* authors explicitly followed Hume in declaring that 'in contriving any system of government ... every man ought to be supposed a *knave*, and to have no other end, than private interest', so that in the absence of public virtue a system pitting the interests of individuals, factions and government departments against one another was necessary (Hume 1985: 42).

Third, despite the ringing endorsement of Enlightenment thinking in the Declaration of Independence, penned by Jefferson – 'we hold these truths to be self-evident, that all men are created equal' – in practice this was clearly belied by the continuing toleration of slavery until the American Civil War of 1861–5, and by the notorious 'three-fifths' clause in the original US constitution. This counted the votes of slaves in states where slave-owning was permitted as 'three-fifths' of the vote of a free man, which not only roundly contradicted the principle of natural equality, but also granted southern slave states extra influence on the House of Representatives and the presidency, by providing them with extra districts and extra electoral college votes (Young 2011: 380).[16] Finally, although it was generally true that the founding fathers were less hostile to the French Revolution than British and French conservatives, its bloodier aspects certainly aroused considerable alarm. Worse, John Adams, the second US president, and perhaps the most conservative of the founding fathers, even on occasion worried that these had been directly caused by the American revolutionaries' example, by encouraging the French to seize political liberty for themselves. As he wrote to Benjamin Rush in 1811: 'have I not been employed in mischief all my days? Did not the American Revolution produce the French Revolution? And did not the French Revolution produce all the calamities and desolation to the human race and the whole globe ever since?' (Adams 1850–6: IX, 635).

Even at the start of the American Revolution, then, there were traces of conservatism. These, however, should not be exaggerated. If anything, they should be regarded as minor elements, or signs of a road largely not taken, rather than as emblematic of a continuous conservative tradition in the United States. For whatever the precedents invoked to justify the break with Britain, the founders still subverted a legal government in a major anti-colonial revolution, ousted loyalist supporters of Britain, 60,000 of whom left the country, and confiscated their property (Young 2018: 43). Furthermore, although the revolution certainly had its limitations, it nevertheless precipitated a radical political transition from a society that had (grudgingly) accepted monarchy to one that became much more infused with republican and democratic values (Wood 1993). And if it is undoubtedly the case that the continuing toleration of slavery by the early American republic represented a significant departure from Enlightenment values, many of the founding fathers, including Jefferson, acceded to this only with considerable reluctance, at least partly due to the impracticality of abolishing slavery in the late eighteenth century (Young 2011: 388). (We must look elsewhere, in other words, for full-throated conservative defences of slavery in the early United States.) In short, therefore, these examples prove that it is mistaken to try and conceptualize the American Revolution as a fully conservative enterprise – despite some early conservative tendencies.

Early conservatism in the United States: Puritanism

Where, then, can we find authentic conservatism in the early United States? Arguably there were two cases of it. First, there was a strong strain of Puritan political thought which had conservative implications, as represented by the Vermont lawyer and politician Nathaniel Niles, particularly in his sermon, the 'Discourse on Liberty' (1774), which drew inspiration from earlier celebrated Puritan authors, such as the seventeenth-century writers John Winthrop and John Cotton. This conception of political thought departed radically from the liberal, Lockean conception of the state which had been espoused by many of the founding fathers, since it rejected the fundamental Lockean premise that good government existed to protect important pre-existing rights (particularly to property) that men had originally possessed, on an individual basis, in the state of nature. In stark contrast, the Puritans argued that human beings originally had no such private interests, but were essentially communal by nature, so that good government existed not to protect individual liberties but to promote the common good, so that 'every one must be required to do all he can that tends to the highest good of the state', as Niles put it (Niles 1983: I, 260). Underpinning this conception was a commitment to the importance of active engagement, of political participation, almost resembling civic republican conceptions of the state; but equally it is important to stress that Puritanism also placed heavy emphasis on the fallen nature of humanity. However virtuous a state might become, ultimately, the Puritans thought, government was only necessary at all because of Adam's fall, because of his original sin. This had three important conservative implications for Niles's political thought.

In the first place, it meant that Niles rejected revolutionary objections to British rule that were based upon Lockean arguments – most notably that by levying taxes without granting representation, the British were violating the legitimacy of their rule, which consisted of an (implied) contract between rulers and ruled. Niles maintained that because human beings were fundamentally put on the earth to be 'stewards' of God's blessings, the legitimacy of *any* government should be measured by the degree to which it promoted Christian values in a sinful world, and not by the degree to which it upheld individual rights – whether to property or anything else. As such, although Niles was critical of British rule before the revolution, and regarded it as illegitimate, an alternative that merely replaced tyranny with 'license', with the reliable satisfaction of private desires, would be no better (Niles 1983: I, 274).

Second, following on from this point, Niles maintained that human beings, as fallen people, were not born free, independent and equal of one another, any more than they are born free, independent and equal of God, or of their parents. As such, he argued, there was a strong obligation on them to respect natural hierarchies, and hence to obey the legitimate authority of the state. It is true that Niles did not stress obedience to the degree that earlier Puritans such as Winthrop had done, and that he emphasized the importance (in general) of respecting majority opinion, and hence of gaining consent for a legitimate government. Nevertheless, the theme of cheerful subjection remained a key feature of his political thought; to quote Niles himself: 'some degree of partial oppression is ... to be expected in every human state, even under the wisest administration' (Niles 1983: I, 265)

Finally, Niles's Puritanism meant that he was not nearly such a strong defender of religious toleration as most of the founding fathers, let alone the atheist Thomas Paine. A key part of the Puritans' political thought had always been to insist on the unassailable rightness of their own theological position, rather than being in favour of wholesale religious toleration, and hence to insist that secular and sacred authority should be intimately linked. And while it is true Niles was more liberal than earlier Puritans, in that he laid greater weight on the freedom of citizens to practise their religion, this right is circumscribed by his insistence that it can be curtailed if 'such a religion ... is inconsistent with the good of the state' (Niles 1983: I, 267–70). Even if fairly liberal in practice, therefore, Niles's position on religious worship is much more conservative in justification.

One source of conservatism in the early United States, then, consisted of Puritanism, and its impact on political thought. By providing a different justification for the legitimacy of the state, and a competing account of human nature, it provided a powerful alternative, at least at a theoretical level, to dominant Lockean liberal and civic republican theories. The second version of conservatism in the USA evolved more slowly, and appeared in the early to mid-nineteenth century due to a many-sided dispute which developed between the northern and southern states of the Union. This was caused partly by differences over the degree to which states (as opposed to the federal government) should have rights over the 'peculiar institution' of slavery, which was found only in southern states, but in particular by a growing economic divergence between the northern states, which were rapidly industrializing and urbanizing, and those in the south, which remained primarily agricultural, organized mostly around large plantations. To some extent, this dispute went back to the very early days of the republic, since, as mentioned above, there had always been a tension between the founding fathers over what constituted genuine freedom, roughly corresponding with the division between north and south. Thus some (like Jefferson) laid more emphasis on the importance of citizens owning land (and hence on the importance of agriculture), while others (like Hamilton) stressed the importance of trading freely within the market.

This tension was significantly exacerbated, however, by the degree of industrialization that had occurred in the north by the middle of the nineteenth century, and the resulting intensification of the debate about what constituted freedom. By 1850, the number of wage labourers in the USA had outstripped the number of slaves, and a significant number of politicians and intellectuals in the north, particularly in the Republican Party, were vigorously advancing the argument that slavery should no longer be tolerated – partly because it was economically inefficient, but also because it violated the fundamental right of all citizens to labour freely. Thus, part of the Republicans' approach was to hammer home an argument ultimately borrowed from Adam Smith that slavery was less economically efficient than free labour, and hence that the south was backward compared to the thriving north, because humans responded better to incentive than to coercion – though they stressed the degree to which capital and labour could be partners in an American context, in contrast to Smith's claims that there would necessarily be a tension between the two sides (Foner 1995: xx–xxi). But equally, if not more importantly, Republicans like Abraham Lincoln argued that slavery was wrong because it infringed the universal natural right to possess the fruits of one's own labour (Foner 1995: xxvi, 29–30). Notwithstanding the considerable ambiguities about what constituted full freedom in practice – since Republicans were ambivalent as to whether labouring freely was sufficient, or whether the possession of land was necessary as well[17] – this constituted a powerful challenge to the traditional practices of the south.

Southern conservatism: John C. Calhoun and George Fitzhugh

In response, southern intellectuals and politicians put forward conservative arguments for upholding the traditional southern way of life, criticizing the liberal, individualistic assumptions that underpinned Republican arguments. This conservative case was put most forcibly by the lawyer, author and journalist George Fitzhugh, in his books *Sociology for the South* (1854) and *Cannibals All! Or, Slaves without Masters* (1857), and by the influential senator and vice president, John C. Calhoun, throughout his career, but particularly in his posthumously published works *Disquisition on Government* (1851) and *Discourse on the Constitution* (1851). To some extent, Fitzhugh and Calhoun echoed Puritan arguments, since they were equally sceptical of Lockean individualism, of viewing society as being essentially constituted of separate agents. However, both went further than the Puritans in their inegalitarianism by arguing not merely in favour of hierarchies in society, but explicitly for the institution of slavery, and by trying to devise constitutional means to protect the traditional hierarchies of the south.

Fitzhugh in particular sought to criticize the Republican conception of liberty, claiming it was a fundamental error to define liberty as the ability of essentially separate individuals to labour freely and to compete in the marketplace. Part of the reason for this was that Fitzhugh, in common with the Puritans, thought it was a mistake to view society as constituted of separate individuals when it was in fact fundamentally organic and naturally hierarchical. But he went further than the Puritans in stressing the degree to which the very survival of modern societies was dependent on government control – so that, to quote Fitzhugh himself, the only right nineteen out of twenty should have was 'to be taken care of and protected, to have guardians, trustees, husbands, or masters; in other words, they have a natural right to be slaves' (Fitzhugh 1960: 69). For Fitzhugh, the fundamental problem with northern, Republican arguments in favour of free labour was that they prioritized liberty in a way that was likely to undermine social order, whereas, on the contrary, liberty was in fact 'an evil which government is intended to correct' (Fitzhugh 1854: 170). But more than that, Fitzhugh argued, Republican arguments were incorrect because they presented a mendacious picture of the status of so-called 'free' labourers, who in reality were simply another kind of slave – 'wage slaves' – with their own kind of oppressors. Far better, he argued, to uphold the southern system, including the institution of slavery, since this was much more capable of catering for the fundamental needs of the great majority of mankind, by maintaining traditional hierarchies and encouraging a certain degree of economic co-operation rather than pure competition (Fitzhugh 1960: 87).

If Fitzhugh focused on criticizing Republican arguments sociologically, Calhoun by contrast concentrated more on finding a political solution to maintain the distinctive culture of the southern states. Certainly, like Fitzhugh, Calhoun was a critic of Republican arguments based upon Lockean analyses of society, arguing in common with him that society was naturally organic, not composed of discrete individuals, and that government, based ultimately on force, was necessary to maintain order. But rather than using this analysis to defend the institution of slavery explicitly, Calhoun sought to protect southern customs by using political means to defend minority rights in a democracy, fearful that the traditions of the south had been menaced by the Tariff Acts of 1828 and 1832 (which had damaged southern cotton interests) and by the rise in popularity of abolitionism (Agresto 2003: 319).

To do this, he looked for means to restrain a tyrannical central government from imposing its laws on the south, rejecting the solution of frequent elections, since although these might make governments more responsive, they would not protect the rights of the minority. Instead, Calhoun argued that each genuine 'interest' within the United States ought to have the right of veto, suggesting that such 'interests' could potentially include different sectors of the American economy (such as the commercial, maritime and agricultural), or individual states within the Union, which would be granted the right to 'nullify' unwanted federal laws within their borders (Calhoun 1953: 23). Calhoun even went so far as to suggest in his *Discourse* that the executive itself could be divided into a dual presidency, with one leader representing northern interests and the other those of the south, the approval of both being necessary to pass legislation

(Calhoun 1953: 100–4). These proposals were to some extent novel, rather than conservative, since they directly contradicted the arguments of most of the founders of the republic (notably Madison), who had contended that such arrangements – rather than generating the mutual respect and compromise that Calhoun predicted – would lead directly to constitutional paralysis, factionalism and anarchy. But this should not obscure the fact that the ultimate ends Calhoun was seeking to achieve were profoundly conservative – the maintenance of a southern way of life, organized fundamentally around plantations, and, of course, the institution of slavery.

Conclusion

What strikes us most, initially at least, when considering conservatism from the French Revolution to 1848 is the sheer variety of its forms. Given the different experiences of France, Britain and the USA in this period, this is perhaps hardly surprising: France underwent a prolonged revolution, the first Napoleonic empire, and various attempts at restoration; the United States established a newly independent country under a new constitution; and Britain was adapting to the developing industrial revolution, economic liberalization and increasingly loud demands for political representation. In view of this, as we have seen, some of the conservative responses produced were very different from one another. The explicit arguments in favour of slavery in the middle of the nineteenth century in the United States, for example, had few analogues in Britain at the time, while Maistre's and Bonald's obsession with the importance of Catholicism for political order had few echoes elsewhere. But there were also some parallels and similarities, particularly by the middle of the nineteenth century – since by then conservatives in all three countries had been forced to confront the challenge of industrialization, the more liberal aspects of the Enlightenment, and the effects of the French Revolution. In Chapter 3, we will examine how conservatism developed from 1848 to the First World War.

3
Conservatism from 1848 to the First World War

New Challenges (1848–1914)

This chapter seeks to examine the development of conservatism between the revolutions of 1848 and the outbreak of the First World War. As we saw in Chapter 2, for some conservatives in the late eighteenth and early nineteenth centuries, the biggest concern was the corrosive effect of the market on traditional institutions; for others it was more the impact of the French Revolution, and especially its doctrine of natural rights and participatory democracy; for others again, it was primarily Enlightenment rationalism, with its tendency to undermine religious faith. To some extent, these themes remained important in the later nineteenth century. There were certainly still conservatives in this era who sought to maintain 'organic' social relationships, to uphold traditional political authority, and to defend (and propagate) traditional religious faith against the encroachments of rationalism. But it is also the case that the challenges conservatives faced changed significantly between 1848 and 1914, causing the forms that conservatism took to evolve and alter. Essentially there were five important new challenges.

First, the nature of the world economy radically altered in the late nineteenth century in four different ways. In the first place, it was technologically much more sophisticated, in terms of both production and distribution. The era famously saw the arrival of a slew of new inventions, including the telephone, the telegraph, the phonograph and the bicycle, and technologically revolutionary industries based on electricity, chemistry and the combustion engine began to flourish (Henry Ford's iconic 'Model T' was first manufactured in 1907). Perhaps even more significantly, across Europe and the USA, the period also witnessed the enormous expansion of previously existing technologies, including vast increases in the production of trains, railway track and ships (Hobsbawm 1987: 52). Secondly, the world economy became far more genuinely global, partly because technological developments improved speeds of travel, but also because countries as diverse as Japan, Russia and the Netherlands all significantly industrialized, with the result that trade in primary products approximately tripled between 1880 and 1913 (Pollard 1985: 492; Lewis 1978: 275). Thirdly, and partly as a result of these changes, the late nineteenth century saw a huge expansion of the mass market, from foodstuffs and clothing to a much wider range of goods, including everything from gas cookers to cinema tickets to the widespread distribution of bananas. Significantly, this led to the creation of a genuinely mass media for the first time – a British newspaper reached a million-copy sale for the first time in the 1890s; a French one did so by around 1900 (Hobsbawm 1987: 53). And finally, as a consequence of such industrialization, urbanization increased faster than ever before, exacerbated by the great land depression of the 1870s and 1880s, so that industrial cities with populations between 50,000 and 100,000 became increasingly common. Crucially, too, cities were inhabited by far more industrial workers than previously – by 1900, roughly two-thirds of their population consisted of manual workers (Bairoch 1978: 91). This in turn stimulated a notable growth in the size of trade unions, particularly in Britain and Germany, though they grew more slowly and haltingly than might have been predicted, largely due to the heterogeneous nature of the working class (Hobsbawm 1987: 115).

Second, partly as a result of such economic changes, the nature of nationalism and imperialism significantly altered in the latter part of the nineteenth century, particularly in Europe. Both were complex phenomena, taking a number of forms, but nevertheless the main patterns of their development were reasonably clear. Nationalism earlier in the century had taken its cue from the ideals of the French Revolution, and therefore tended to be a self-consciously liberal and modernizing movement, with the central aim of establishing viable nation-states, with the requisite economy, technology, state organization and military force to sustain themselves (Bayley and Biagini 2008). However, from the 1870s and 1880s, nationalism tended to become transformed into a more aggressive movement that was generally explicitly organized around ethnic and linguistic identities, primarily as a consequence of the uprooting of traditional communities due to emigration and urbanization. This uprooting had two reinforcing effects. Negatively, it encouraged a strong feeling of nostalgia for a lost community and culture amongst those uprooted, which tended to emphasize the importance of a continuing common identity, based around language and ethnicity. More positively, it encouraged those uprooted to invest their feelings of loyalty in the 'imagined community' of the nation-state, not least because the latter offered the prospect of security after the breakdown of traditional hierarchies. This tendency was reinforced by nation-states themselves, which moved to provide mass elementary education for the first time as a means to bind countries together (Hobsbawm 1987: 148–50).

Likewise, imperialism, although hardly an unknown phenomenon before the 1870s, and indeed on some definitions as old as the ancient world, significantly changed in the period between 1880 and 1914, since it was prosecuted much more aggressively and affected a much larger part of the globe. Thus, in this period, about a quarter of the globe's land surface was redistributed as colonies amongst half a dozen states, most notably in Africa and the Pacific, with Britain increasing its territories by approximately 4 million square miles, France by around 3.5 million, and Germany, Italy and Belgium roughly 1 million each. This occurred due to a combination of economic, political and cultural factors. Economically, as we have already seen, the late nineteenth century saw a huge expansion of the mass market in developed countries, along with technological developments which allowed for much quicker travel to develop new markets, and hence the creation of a genuinely globalized economy. But it was the *competition* for these new markets that drove mass colonization, coupled with an increasing tendency by imperial governments, after the 'Great Depression' of the 1870s and 1880s, to protect their markets by tariffs, such that these economic developments became inextricably linked to political calculations (Hobsbawm 1987: 59, 67). And since colonies increasingly came to be seen, particularly by ambitious and newly unified countries like Germany, as status symbols in and of themselves, this exacerbated imperial tensions even further, while back at home colonial powers revelled in showing off the exotic fruits of their overseas possessions in elaborate exhibitions and imperial jubilees (McAleer and MacKenzie 2015; Geppert 2010).

Third, partly as a consequence of these developments, the nature of the state in Western Europe and the USA changed significantly between 1848 and 1914, for three related reasons. In the first place, due to a rising population, industrialization and urbanization, governments were inclined to grant more members of society the vote, to gain the loyalty of new groups at a time of uncertainty for older hierarchies. This process was patchy and incomplete, with women being almost universally excluded from voting until the twentieth century; black voters in the United States often being prevented from voting in practice, even after their admission to suffrage at the end of civil war; only around 40 per cent of male voters able to vote in Britain in the Edwardian period; and French voters subject to various forms of manipulation, despite the granting of universal manhood suffrage in 1848. Nevertheless, the process was significant (Hobsbawm 1987: 85–6; Garrard 2006). Secondly, partly to educate the working men gaining the vote, but also to foster greater national integration and provide more trained workers for the industrialized economy, the state became much more heavily involved in educating the public, particularly after 1870, with Germany spending around 12 per cent of the state budget on public education, England 10 per cent and France 8 per cent in 1901 (Leonhard 2006: 145). Finally, in response to the social problems caused by rapid industrialization and urbanization, and to some extent trade union pressure, governments from the 1880s onwards began to enact schemes to improve social conditions and provide basic welfare benefits, including pensions, unemployment benefits and compensation for industrial accidents. While these schemes tended to be relatively modest in scope, particularly compared to the more comprehensive welfare states created after the 1930s Depression and the Second World War, they nevertheless represented a significant increase in the role of the state compared to the earlier nineteenth century (Leonhard 2006: 146–7; Mommsen and Mock 1981).

Fourth, more intellectually, the later nineteenth century saw important changes in the way in which human nature and society were conceptualized, with social and political theorists tending to put greater stress on the historical development of societies and the potentially mutable nature of human beings. To some extent, of course, such arguments were hardly unprecedented – as we saw in Chapter 2, in the late eighteenth century various Scottish Enlightenment theorists, most notably Adam Smith, had argued that human societies had fundamentally changed due to developments in economic production, as hunter gatherers had been progressively succeeded by pastoral, arable and finally commercial civil societies. Furthermore, in the earlier nineteenth century, influential Idealist and positivist theorists, notably G. W. F. Hegel and Auguste Comte, had maintained that human societies systematically progressed through various eras, the increasing social and political sophistication of each era being directly related in their theories to the increasing mental sophistication of its inhabitants. Nevertheless, the stress political and social theorists placed on historical development clearly intensified in the later nineteenth century, for three reasons.

In the first place, the period saw the establishment of a genuinely professional approach to historical study in many Western countries, with the creation and systematic use of archives for the first time, and the appearance of scholarly journals, such as the *Revue Historique* (1876) and the *English Historical Review* (1886) (Lambert 2020). Secondly, this systematization also spread to related disciplines such as sociology, the key 'founding fathers' of which, including Emile Durkheim and Karl Marx, were far more likely to undertake genuine historical research to support their conclusions, in contrast to those who had influenced them, like Comte and Adam Smith. Finally, intersecting with these developments, later nineteenth-century social and political thought was significantly influenced by theories of 'social evolution'. This was primarily due to the publication of Charles Darwin's enormously influential work *The Origin of Species* in 1859, with its theory of natural selection – although alternative theories of evolution had already been suggested earlier in the century, notably by Jean-Baptiste Lamarck and Herbert Spencer. But there is no question that the new focus on social evolutionary theory concentrated attention on the developmental nature of mankind, and indeed on the potential links that humans had with animals. As such, one major consequence of the popularity of social evolutionary theories was an intensified interest in classifying different 'races', with some theorists, such as the zoologist Ernst Haeckel, claiming that one could arrange them in a hierarchy, with the most primitive regarded as the most 'animalistic', and the most developed as the most 'civilized' (Haeckel 1876: II, 307–9, 325, 363–5). Equally, however, the claim that humans were descended directly from animals also led to concerns, particularly by the turn of the twentieth century, that humanity's primitive instincts remained powerful, and were especially liable to reappear at moments of stress or in wartime.

Finally, conservatives in the later nineteenth century were confronted by progressive ideologies that had significantly mutated. Earlier in the century, as we saw in Chapter 2, the Enlightenment had already inspired a number of liberal and radical challenges to traditional hierarchies and ways of living. In particular, liberal demands for greater political and economic freedom, often justified by the assertion that all individuals have fundamentally equal reasoning abilities, proved a significant challenge for conservatives, as did the argument that granting greater liberty would enable developed societies to progress. This remained the case in the later nineteenth century, as liberals sought to wrest privileges away from traditional authorities, especially the aristocracy and the church. But such challenges intensified in this period, as progressive political thinkers reacted to the changing economic, political and intellectual circumstances by arguing for more radical positions, envisaging, variously, greater state intervention, redistribution of property, and even sometimes violent revolution. Thus, for example, by the early twentieth century, 'new' liberals such as L. T. Hobhouse and J. A. Hobson in Britain argued in favour of greater state intervention to secure liberty, partly because they thought that economic intervention was necessary to prevent monopolies forming (hence creating inequality of opportunity), but also because they argued that individuals were not truly free unless they were given genuine opportunities to flourish socially and economically (Hobson 1974: 4; Hobhouse 1911: 163).

Alongside these radical liberal positions, the later nineteenth and early twentieth centuries also saw socialist ideas grow significantly in popularity. In particular, Karl Marx's writings provided a powerful new set of arguments against the established order, by contending that all social and political relationships were, in fact, fundamentally based upon whoever had control of the means of production within a society, and that under capitalism there was inevitably an unresolved tension between those who had control of those 'means' and those who did not. According to this socialist argument, claims that political legitimacy rested upon an ability to maximize individual freedom (as liberals contended), or to maintain a harmonious society based upon a well-ordered hierarchy (as conservatives claimed), missed the point since they ignored this fundamental reality (Marx 1977: 289). Instead, Marx argued, the only way to ensure genuine emancipation was to equalize access to the 'means of production', a task he argued could only be achieved through revolution, since the ruling class, which under capitalism was primarily the bourgeoisie, would not relinquish its control voluntarily. As well as issuing a direct challenge to liberal and conservative theories of political legitimacy, Marx's position also provided a powerful alternative analysis of human history, arguing that historical development was essentially driven, materialistically, by the contradictions between the justifications of a particular political system and its underlying economic reality, so that any type of social organization, other than communism, was inherently unstable (Marx and Engels 1965: 51).

Marx's arguments did not, however, exhaust all the

possibilities that late nineteenth-century socialism had to offer. There were other socialist thinkers who supported Marx's ultimate goal of creating a genuinely 'free' society – defined by Marx as a society with a sufficient degree of equality and sense of community for individuals to labour freely – but denied that a revolution was necessary for this to be achieved. Thus, at the turn of the twentieth century in Germany, the revisionist Marxist thinker Eduard Bernstein argued in favour of a more evolutionary route to a socialist society, contending that capitalism was liable to give way to socialism more easily than Marx had foreseen, so that instituting a genuinely participatory democracy was much more important in achieving a genuinely equal society than Marx had considered it to be (Bernstein 1961: 147–61). Conversely, in Britain – where, as in the USA, Marx's version of socialism was generally unpopular – Fabian socialists such as Beatrice and Sidney Webb stressed the need for experts to ensure administrative efficiency in government. If, like Bernstein, they emphasized the importance of full suffrage (so that the interests of the working classes were truly represented), the Fabians were more elitist in believing that only a fairly dirigiste state could ensure that a society was run effectively, with its resources allocated rationally (Webb and Webb 1897: I, 32; Neill 2006: 217–22).

Confronted by this range of new challenges it was perhaps unsurprising that conservatives in the later nineteenth century reacted in a wide variety of ways. Indeed, such was the diversity of their response – notably over how enthusiastically to advocate capitalism, how keenly to embrace imperialism, and how much state intervention to welcome – that some scholars have claimed that conservatism actually became incoherent in these years, or at best irreparably splintered into different types. W. H. Greenleaf, for example, argued that conservatism in these years became inherently divided between libertarian, anti-statist thinkers, intent on resisting government interference and upholding the free market, and those who remained more paternalist, keen to retain traditional hierarchies and values, and to aid the poor through state intervention (Greenleaf 1983–7: II, 189–95). But such analyses have only a limited use, since they underplay the continuing importance of the 'core' concepts that sustain conservatism, as explored in Chapter 1, namely a commitment to managing change cautiously, and a belief that ultimately individual actions have to be viewed as subject to an 'extra-human' order. Furthermore, much of the diversity in the conservative response can be explained by the tendency of the ideology to 'mirror' its opponents proactively, misidentifying its core concepts either consciously or unconsciously, so as to produce an effective ideological alternative. Broadly speaking, conservatives made three main responses to the challenges outlined above, each of which we will now consider in turn.

Conservative Response I: An Embrace of the Market

First, conservatives such as W. H. Mallock, Hugh Cecil and Herbert Spencer in Britain, and W. G. Sumner in the United States, responded to the challenges of the later nineteenth century primarily by addressing the advent of socialism and progressive liberalism in theory, and the associated growth of the state in practice. To do this, they sought to colonize territory previously held by early nineteenth-century liberal political theorists, arguing in favour of the inviolability of private property, the importance of a free market, and the benefits of self-help and voluntary assistance rather than state provision of welfare services. Crucially, their advocacy of these ideas tended to be underpinned by a commitment to the core conservative concepts of controlled change and an extra-human order, and formulated in partisan opposition to particular progressive concepts, such as equality, hence identifying them definitively as conservative rather than liberal theorists. Despite broad similarities, however, these thinkers also differed importantly from one another in terms of their fundamental philosophical beliefs and to some extent their normative arguments.

Thus, taking Mallock first, we find an author and pamphleteer who sought to adapt to the changing social and political situation by substituting a defence of capitalism and industrial entrepreneurship for his earlier support for a more traditional hierarchical order based upon land. Although in his early work Mallock had defended the aristocracy against what he saw as the selfishness and socially irresponsible radicalism of the industrial middle classes – and then, in his novel, *The Old Order Changes* (1886), briefly suggested that the aristocratic virtue of *noblesse oblige* could be transferred to morally transformed industrialists – he subsequently became a firm defender of industrial capitalism (Ford 1974: 318–19). In other words, rather than continuing to be a conservative devoted to defending traditional institutions, Mallock became dedicated above all to disproving socialism, and to finding economic, even scientific, justifications for why social stability required a productive elite. Conservatism thus became, for him, 'the material well-being of the people first, and everything else afterwards' (Mallock 1884: 702).

How did Mallock believe such material well-being could be secured? Key to his position was that although many factors contributed to production and wealth, including land, labour and capital, crucial above all to economic success was individual entrepreneurial ability. This was, he argued, both the creator of all capital and the reason for 'all progress in production' (Mallock 1893: 154–5). As such, he was explicitly seeking to combat the argument put forward by Marxian socialists (but ultimately derived from Scottish Enlightenment thinkers like Adam Smith) that the ultimate source of all productive value was labour, by arguing that to include technological invention and entrepreneurial expertise within such a category was a fundamental mistake, even a deceit. Rather, Mallock insisted, such abilities were entirely separate, and possessed only by a minority in each generation, so that progress would always depend upon maintaining a propertied elite capable of innovating (Mallock 1908: 34; 1898: 120). This in turn meant that the state should refrain, as far as possible, from interfering in the economy, since without the genuine test of market conditions, in which the inefficient failed and the efficient succeeded, no real progress could be guaranteed. A state-employed official, for example, would have security of tenure, and could only be dismissed by politicians – who might themselves easily be swayed by bribery or public opinion (Mallock 1908: 69). It is important to note that Mallock did not draw the conclusion from his elitist argument that mass democracy should be resisted altogether – unlike some of the reactionaries and pessimists that we will discuss later in this chapter, he did not believe that allowing democracy would inevitably mean that the state would bend to every whim of the masses (Ford 1974: 326).[1] Nevertheless, although Mallock insisted that his economic elite was ultimately there to serve the people, his position represented a strident rejection of socialism, and in particular of its claims that wealth was communally created, and could easily be distributed more equitably.

The second example of a conservative thinker who sought to uphold individual liberties against the state in the later nineteenth century was Herbert Spencer, already mentioned as a highly influential evolutionary theorist in the Victorian period, and coiner of the phrase 'the survival of the fittest'. At first sight, categorizing Spencer as a conservative might seem surprising. Not an intellectual associated with the Conservative Party in the mid-Victorian period, Spencer had on the contrary often been grouped with liberal intellectuals such as J. S. Mill and T. H. Green. He supported, for example, the liberal attempt to prosecute Governor Eyre in 1865 for his brutality in putting down a colonial rebellion in Jamaica, against conservative opposition which included the philosopher and social commentator Thomas Carlyle. But by the time Spencer came to write *The Man versus the State* in 1884, he had become deeply concerned that the growth of the state in the late Victorian period was in danger of threatening individual liberties, and his position became increasingly conservative. To quote Spencer himself: 'if the present drift of things continues, it may ... really happen that the Tories will be defenders of liberties which the Liberals, in pursuit of what they think popular welfare, trample under foot' (Spencer 1994: 79). Ultimately this was because Spencer's political position was derived from a version of evolutionary theory which claimed that all phenomena, including the social and political as much as the physical and biological, tended to develop to become more complex, integrated and heterogeneous. This, he argued, meant that modern societies had become more differentiated, full of individuals carrying out mutually beneficial but discrete activities – as opposed to more primitive ones which were more homogeneous and bellicose – and that it was therefore vital to respect the freedom of individuals in order for further progress to occur (Spencer 1994: 171–3; Meadowcroft 1995: 74–7).[2] As such, Spencer argued, it was essential that individuals be protected from the illegitimate interference of an overmighty state, whose function should be limited on the domestic front to preventing crime and enforcing contracts, and protecting society from external aggression when it came to foreign affairs (Spencer 1994: 163–4; Meadowcroft 1995: 81). By contrast, any attempt by the state at directly ameliorating poverty, or protecting citizens from the consequences of their own poor choices, was in danger of hindering the progress of society as a whole by encouraging weakness, thereby interfering with the beneficent process of evolution whereby individuals become better fitted to their circumstances and integrated with one another (Spencer 1994: 167, 128–9).

It is worth stressing how genuinely conservative Spencer's argument was. For what looked ostensibly like a relatively progressive position, advocating individual responsibility and the importance of social evolution, was in fact one that had three key conservative features. First, Spencer crucially argued that evolutionary change was a process that occurred independently of rational control, in stark contrast to more progressive evolutionary theorists, like Hobhouse and Hobson, who claimed that human reason could be used to guide its future development. As such, 'evolution' in Spencer's thought functions in a highly conservative manner, as an 'extra-human' phenomenon which constrains rationality and individual decision-making rather than supporting them (Freeden 1996: 374). Second, since any attempt at conscious intervention in the evolutionary process, particularly by the state, was almost bound to have negative consequences in modernity, according to Spencer, this limited the degree to which rapid beneficial change was possible. And third, this cautiously conservative approach to change is reinforced by the fact that although Spencer's position shares certain features with liberalism (especially in the desire to maximize individual liberty, which is why his thought is often labelled 'libertarian'), his arguments importantly differ from those of earlier liberals by decoupling the concept of 'liberty' from that of moral progress (Freeden 1996: 295–6). Thus according to liberal theorists like J. S. Mill, quite as much as Hobhouse and Hobson, one of the key reasons for increasing personal liberty was to enable individuals to become better citizens, to acquire a good 'character'. For Spencer, by contrast, no such moral improvement could be expected, since 'the defective natures of citizens will show themselves in the bad acting of whatever social structure they are arranged into' (Spencer 1994: 105). For Spencer then, quite in keeping with conservative thought, change had to be managed carefully, since however much modern societies could provide greater liberty, they could not improve the nature of mankind, or at least not in any direct or rapid manner.

If, in Britain and continental Europe, Spencer's arguments in *The Man versus the State* were in general becoming less popular, compared with the increasingly influential progressive ideologies of new liberalism and socialism, in the USA they found a much more receptive audience. In what was an era of buccaneering capitalism in the United States, powerful business leaders like Andrew Carnegie and John D. Rockefeller proved highly responsive to Spencer's arguments, finding in his work theoretical justifications for their own worldview, and Spencer's influence only grew after the triumphal tour of the United States he made in 1882.[3]

Probably the most important advocate of all for Spencer's ideas in the United States was the Yale academic and pioneer sociologist W. G. Sumner, who defined 'social good' materialistically as 'economic power, material prosperity, and group strength for war' (McCloskey 1951: 46). Arguing, like Spencer, that direct attempts by the state to improve social conditions were doomed to failure, since they merely interfered with the beneficent processes of capitalist competition, Sumner claimed to be speaking on behalf of 'the forgotten man', 'the clean, quiet, virtuous, domestic citizen who pays his debts and his taxes and is never to be heard of outside his little circle', who was menaced by such progressive, statist, schemes (Sumner 1963: 123). As such, again following Spencer, Sumner offered only wary support for democracy, arguing that although it was the only system of government suitable for the United States, nevertheless it almost inevitably led to reformist demands that threatened the autonomy of 'the forgotten man'. But he also deviated from Spencer somewhat, in raising questions about the way capitalism in the United States worked, and arguing that it had become afflicted by 'jobbery', namely by attempts to gain financially by illicit means. For Sumner, this tendency within capitalism, previously restrained somewhat by aristocracies, was now a major problem (Sumner 1963: 241). Nevertheless he still maintained, like Spencer, that any interference in the process of capitalist competition would be disastrous – despite the fact that American capitalism itself was, in reality, becoming more corporatist and less individualist at the end of the nineteenth century, quite apart from any direct intervention by the state. Such was the power and popularity of this brand of capitalist conservatism that it was arguably intellectually dominant in the USA well into the 1920s, until the disastrous Wall Street Crash of 1929.

In contrast to the position of Spencer and Sumner, the final type of conservatism that sought to defend liberty against the new encroachments of the modern state in the late nineteenth and early twentieth centuries drew on more familiar Burkean arguments, emphasizing the continued compatibility of tradition, religion and the free market. Probably the most important representative of this form of conservatism was the younger son of the British prime minister Lord Salisbury, the politician and theorist Lord Hugh Cecil, whose work *Conservatism* (1912) formed part of the same series on political ideologies as Hobhouse's *Liberalism*. To some extent, Cecil's position resembled that of Spencer and Mallock. Like them, he objected to much of the new economic intervention by the state, on the grounds that it very often did more harm than good. He was, for example, suspicious of any attempt at regulating trade and labour (beyond setting basic working conditions for workers who could not protect themselves, like women and children), let alone expanding state-run industries, which he claimed ran the risk of driving out private capital, inflating the number of public functionaries, straining public finances, and making the tax burden unbearable (Cecil 1912: 188; 1908: 43–8).

More fundamentally, like the other two theorists, Cecil refused to give ground to progressive arguments that inequalities in society were severe enough to constitute an injustice that the state should remove. On the contrary, he argued, justice did not demand equality, but merely that no one be 'injured or cheated', so that in practice existing property arrangements should usually be respected. He also agreed with Spencer and Sumner that infringements of personal liberty should be avoided, since otherwise individuals would lack the ability to make moral choices, and hence to develop their characters for the better (Cecil 1912: 168; 1910: 10, 17). But despite these similarities, Cecil's conclusions rested on very different foundations. For him, as for Burke, the state's authority and legitimacy ultimately rested on its being the 'trustee' of a beneficent tradition, and upholding 'tradition' for Cecil, just as for Burke, was inextricably linked to the preservation of religion – political decisions, he argued, should be judged against 'Christian morals as revealed in the New Testament' (Cecil 1912: 75, 165).

This had three important implications for Cecil's brand of conservatism. In the first place, it meant that the state should not, as in Spencer's conception, be viewed as a purely 'external' body exercising force, whose only legitimate function in industrial society was to guarantee and maximize the freedom of individuals (and their safety from foreign threats). Rather, the state according to Cecil should be conceptualized as an entity which represents the inherited collective moral wisdom of 'the nation', and therefore as capable of taking positive action to realize projects that are consonant with such shared moral values (Cecil 1912: 54; Meadowcroft 1995: 105–7). In the second place, following on from this, it meant that Cecil's state had considerably more freedom for manoeuvre than Spencer's. While for Spencer the only justification for state intervention was to ensure a correspondence between the conduct and consequences of individual actions, for Cecil the state could (and should) do whatever was necessary to ensure order and social stability. As such, he was much more open to the idea of supporting traditional poor relief, or even new projects like pensions and national insurance, if these were necessary to maintaining order – provided they were not justified on the basis that they were needed to correct actual *injustices*, as progressives argued (Cecil 1912: 177–9, 186). On the same basis, Cecil was open to cautious reform of the constitution to increase the state's legitimacy, including reform of the House of Lords to ensure more equal representation of the parties, votes for women (albeit still with a property qualification), and even experiments with referenda and proportional representation (Meadowcroft 1995: 100–1). Finally, unlike for Spencer, for whom religion was merely an atavistic vestige of more primitive societies, a form of social solidarity unnecessary in modernity, for Cecil religion remained of vital importance for the state. If the rupturing of religious uniformity in modern times meant that the denomination of Christianity to be endowed would vary according to region, nevertheless the importance of the state retaining a link to the church could hardly be overestimated (Cecil 1912: 103–4). Without that, Cecil believed, in contrast to Spencer and Mallock, the state would not make genuinely moral decisions, in accordance with the best instincts of its people. Here, as elsewhere, Cecil sought to update what he took to be a Burkean version of conservatism for the early twentieth century.

Conservative Response II: Nationalism and Imperialism

If some conservatives, particularly in Britain and the USA, reacted to the changes in the second half of the nineteenth century by opposing greater state intervention and advocating individual liberty to a greater extent than they had before, colonizing ideological territory that liberals had previously occupied, a second group of conservatives reacted more radically, particularly in continental Europe. Apprehensive in varying degrees about the impact of urbanization, secularization and mass democracy after 1848, they were also to some extent inspired by the failure of the famous revolutions of that year to secure full reforms in France, the Habsburg Empire and the German and Italian states (amongst others). For despite the radicals' initial successes in securing greater democratic representation, freedom of assembly and freedom of the press, and some longer-term achievements in abolishing serfdom in Austria and establishing representative democracy in the Netherlands, they were generally unsuccessful in overturning the established European political order. This was primarily because, as conservatives increasingly observed, some of the revolting groups (like peasants and artisans) were as much reacting against the effects of liberal capitalism as they were in favour of political radicalism; by contrast, it tended to be middle-class professionals and intellectuals who were most zealous for reform (Evans and von Strandmann 2000; Sperber 2005).

In response, such conservatives sought to capitalize on such worries, not just by promising to safeguard the property rights of such groups against the threat of socialism, but also by harnessing nationalism and imperialism to combat progressive ideologies. In this they were aided by the developments outlined earlier – namely that nationalism was mutating into a more aggressive ethnic-linguistic phenomenon, and that imperialism was also becoming more belligerent, stimulated by increased global competition. Conservatives of this second sort differed from one another in terms of how easy it would be to use nationalism and imperialism for their purposes, since there was an obvious danger that the social and political pressures of these movements were likely to have a major impact on traditional elites, as well as other unforeseeable consequences. Nevertheless, they thought the opportunities outweighed the risks (Goldman 2011: 695–7). We will examine briefly how conservatism of this type operated in three different countries, namely Germany, France and Britain.

Initially, then, let us consider how conservatives in Germany sought to harness nationalism to their advantage after 1848. In some ways, they faced an unfavourable environment. For despite the emphatic failure of the 1848 revolution to overturn the established order, liberals in Germany retained a popular and viable programme for unification, based upon promoting constitutional reform within each state, while removing tariff barriers across Germany by extending Prussia's 1833 customs union, with the eventual aim of producing a newly unified federation. Furthermore, in the later nineteenth and early twentieth centuries, once Germany had been unified and the franchise extended, conservatives faced the challenge of an increasingly popular social democratic party, which, at least on paper, supported Marxism. In fact, however, conservatives were able to reform their ideology successfully, and in practice resist the pressure being put on the Junkers, the landed nobility, to relinquish power. This was partly because the Junkers themselves, as highly competent bureaucrats, soldiers and estate-managers, were far from being indolent parasites. But it was above all due to the efforts of Otto von Bismarck, Prussian nobleman and first Chancellor of Germany, who successfully ensured the continuing dominance of traditional elites by forming tactical alliances at home and winning significant (if limited) wars abroad. Infamous for arguing that Germany could be united only by 'blood and iron', rather than by conceding to liberal reforms, Bismarck, as Prussian foreign minister, first manipulated Austria into war in 1866, and then France in 1870–1, winning both conflicts, and ensuring that Wilhelm I was proclaimed emperor of Germany on the back of these successes.

At home, Bismarck's strategy was classically conservative: rather than simply resisting all liberal reforms, he sought to manage and neutralize them. Thus, for example, rather than resisting universal suffrage, he rendered it relatively toothless by ensuring that the upper house (the Bundesrat) would be dominated by Prussia, and that military budgets would be free from parliamentary control – while also granting a limited welfare state. Even when Bismarck was forced to resign in 1890, the system he designed remained in operation, at least domestically. A powerful conservative alliance of aristocrats, generals and bureaucrats remained in power, so that despite the huge extent of industrialization in these years, and the increasing popularity of the social democratic party, the degree of liberalization in Germany was limited (Weiss 1977: 78–84; Mommsen 2011: 421–30). Indeed, such was Bismarck's success that German conservative theorists, most notably the historian Heinrich von Treitschke, were inspired to base their arguments for an ideal state on Bismarck's creation. What Bismarck had largely achieved, Treitschke felt, was a state designed to preserve old institutions and values, such as the patriarchal family, traditional rural society and self-sacrificial military virtue – rather than acceding to the temptations of modern consumerism and the demand that the modern state should serve the masses. But if anything Treitschke went even further than Bismarck, arguing that war was an end in itself (since it helped to combat selfish individualism and promoted heroic virtue), that there was a strict hierarchy of different races (with the 'Teutons' and 'Anglo-Saxons' at the top), and that the Jews in particular were responsible for all kinds of vices – including socialism and the 1848 revolutions. Radical conservatives like Treitschke thus transformed Bismarck's conservative legacy into something much more crudely imperialist and authoritarian, combined with an anti-Semitism that had ominous implications for German history in the twentieth century (Weiss 1977: 84–9; Dorpalen 1957).

Turning to France, to some extent there were similar developments to those in Germany in the late nineteenth century, although the situation was more complicated. Until the 1880s, intense patriotism had been associated at least as much with the Jacobin phase of the 1789 revolution, and with the liberalizing nationalism of Napoleon, as it had been with the conservative Right. Furthermore, the Third Republic had only come into being after the military defeat of Napoleon III's Second Empire in the Franco-Prussian war, and the failure of the Right to restore one of the candidates for the monarchy in 1871. As such, the context seemed considerably less promising for conservatives than in Germany. Nevertheless, by the turn of the century, there were three reasons why various forms of conservatism were in fact flourishing.

In the first place, as in Germany, the popularity of social Darwinism opened the way for the expression of explicitly racist arguments, and France produced one of the most influential exponents of these, namely Joseph de Gobineau. In his widely read *Essai sur L'Inégalité des Races Humaines* (1853–5), Gobineau argued against democracy on the basis that it would encourage 'racial mixing', and hence the intellectual degeneration of the 'higher' races (Biddiss 1970: 170, 172). Second, the Catholic Church retained considerable power and prestige in France, and was a vital support to the forces of conservatism; Sacré-Cœur, the church of the Sacred Heart of Jesus in Paris, was, for example, explicitly conceived as an embodiment of the conservative moral order, to atone for the immorality of the socialist Paris Commune of 1871. Finally, although the founding of the Third Republic was a setback for conservatives, it did not represent any kind of final defeat for conservatism, or even for royalism. The republic remained deeply split between different ideological factions: liberals, socialists and conservatives; republicans and monarchists; Catholics and freethinkers. The weak and divided nature of the Third Republic was partially revealed in the 1880s, when its unpopularity and corruption almost led to its overthrow by General Boulanger in 1889 (before the general lost his nerve). But it was above all the trauma of the Dreyfus case that exposed the republic's problems (Gildea 1996: 21–3; Seager 1969; Cahm 1996). What began as a relatively simple (if scurrilous) case of corruption – after the French army captain Alfred Dreyfus was imprisoned on a false charge of spying for Germany in 1894 – ended up convulsing some of the most fundamental institutions of the republic. It became clear that the underlying cause of Dreyfus's conviction was the dislike on the part of conservative, Catholic army officers for his Jewishness, and their willingness to resort to forgery and corruption to keep him in jail. The case galvanized the liberals, socialists and intellectuals who supported Dreyfus, including the sociologist Emile Durkheim and the novelist Emile Zola, whose famous open letter to the president of the republic, 'J'Accuse...!', electrified the French public and led to Zola's own prosecution (Gildea 1996: 53–4; Jennings 2011: 448–63). But it also stimulated the opposition, the 'anti-Dreyfusards', and if this group contained some republicans, like Paul Déroulède, the majority of its members were conservative nationalists. What did they believe?

To get a flavour of what French conservative nationalists believed at the turn of the twentieth century, we will briefly examine the work of two influential theorists with overlapping positions: the writer and critic Ferdinand Brunetière, and the journalist and politician Maurice Barrès. Both, picking up conservative themes we saw in Chapter 2, argued for the importance of tradition against rationalism, for collective religious identity against individualism, and hence also for anti-Semitism – on the basis that Jews, being quintessentially rootless and venal, would be unable, or at the very least unlikely, to appreciate the worth of such arguments. Brunetière, for his part, argued that modern individualists in general, and the Dreyfusards in particular, were in danger of undermining what was fundamental to France's spirit. That spirit, Brunetière argued in a variety of works, but particularly in *Les Ennemis de L'Ame Française* (1899), consisted of three mutually reinforcing traditions. First, there was the army, which had to be defended against Dreyfusard attacks, since having a strong military force was vital for the continuing existence of the nation. Second, France's great literary tradition had to be maintained and nourished, since great literature had given France a 'truthful expression, a durable expression, an immortal expression'. This, Brunetière claimed, meant resisting modernist obsessions with 'art for art's sake' or with Protestant notions of 'individual salvation', and upholding the role of art as offering a moral message for the community. Finally, and most importantly, it was vital to defend Catholicism, for 'in the way that Protestantism is England and "orthodoxy" is Russia, so France is Catholicism'. Catholicism above all, Brunetière claimed, provided an unbroken tradition that helped to sustain all that was best in France, and although it was entirely possible to be non-Catholic and still genuinely French, those who actively sought to undermine Catholicism were excluded by definition (Brunetière 1899: 57–8; Jennings 2011: 453–4).

Barrès largely agreed with this diagnosis, but his articulation of nationalist conservatism was harsher and more overtly political. Famous for writing a novel, *Les Déracines* (1897), criticizing those who had become alienated or 'uprooted' from the concrete experience of being French by advocating abstract, universal, individualist ideals over time-honoured traditions and actual lived experience, Barrès used this critique to attack intellectuals as 'the enemy of society', likely to lead the unwary into decadence. And if anything his contempt for Jews was even greater, since they lacked a country in the true sense that the French understood France. For them, France was not the country of their soil and their ancestors, but 'only a place where they find greatest profit', as he put it in his *Scènes et Doctrines du Nationalisme* (1902) (Barrès 1906: 152). There was in response, Barrès argued, a clear need for a political programme to strengthen the French nation. This would mean tightening up nationality laws so as to reduce the role of foreigners in French politics. The economic interests of French workers should be secured against what Barrès referred to as the 'financial feudality' of Protestants and the 'kingdom of Israel'. And every French family should be granted a 'corner of the land' so as to genuinely anchor them to the soil of France – since, as Barrès put it, 'our salvation lies in ceasing to be uprooted and scattered individuals' (Jennings 2011: 455–6). For Barrès, therefore, there could be no half measures; his version of conservatism entailed a complete rejection of both cosmopolitan socialism and economic liberalism alike.

Conservative Response III: Nostalgia, Radicalism and Pessimism

If conservatives embracing nationalism and imperialism were intent on maintaining traditional values and existing elites, nevertheless, almost by necessity, they were also obliged to update and adapt them. However much an imperialist like Treitschke was seeking to protect the traditional family and the values of the Prussian aristocracy, he was also advocating something new – namely a German colonial empire, which even Bismarck thought was too much of an innovation. This vision remained fundamentally conservative because it sought to manage change rather than embrace a new liberal or socialist order; nevertheless there were aspects of it that were genuinely innovatory – and overall the vision remained relatively optimistic. By contrast, a third group of conservatives responded far more pessimistically to the onset of modernity, with some reacting particularly strongly to the effects of the market economy and international capitalism, while others worried more about the onset of mass democracy. The former type tended to be far more critical of liberal individualism than of socialism – particularly if it was a variant of a socialism that stressed the importance of community rather than state redistribution

– since their primary concern was the damage they felt the market had done to traditional communities and pre-modern values. (Indeed, some of these thinkers have even been identified as socialists rather than conservatives; the claim being made here, however, is not that they were unambiguously conservative but that insofar as their thought genuinely conformed to the dictates of conservative ideology, they are better identified as conservative rather than socialist thinkers.) The latter type of conservative tended to worry that mass democracy would ineluctably empower the masses to demand an aggressive and confiscatory socialism, with the consequence that traditional structures and hierarchies would be swept away. As examples for the former type, we will briefly examine the Victorian thinkers Thomas Carlyle and John Ruskin in Britain, and for the latter, Henry Adams in the United States.

Taking Carlyle first, then, we encounter an influential, if idiosyncratic, Scottish thinker in the middle of the nineteenth century who was deeply concerned about the negative effects of liberal capitalism on society and politics, which he ultimately put down to the unfortunate impact the Enlightenment had had on religion and philosophy. Despite the positive effects of the Enlightenment in stimulating critical thought, Carlyle argued, it had also caused fundamental problems, both in theory and in practice, by encouraging the misapplication of instrumental thinking beyond scientific phenomena to those that concerned human action and motivation. On a theoretical level, because such instrumental thinking, which Carlyle referred to as 'the science of mechanics', had been wrongly applied in philosophy, it had encouraged the explanation of human behaviour with reference to external stimuli rather than moral motivation – thus causing the ascendancy of utilitarianism as a theory of human conduct. In practical terms, it had led to an overemphasis on improving the material needs of a growing population, rather than ministering to their moral, religious and spiritual needs – and hence provided support for economic theories that maximized profit at all cost. As Carlyle put it: 'thus is the Body-politic more than ever worshipped and tended; but the Soul-politic less than ever' (Carlyle 1893: III, 239–40). The result was a situation where the working classes had justified complaints about their living conditions, as Carlyle admitted in his text *Chartism* (1839), but where these complaints could only ultimately be addressed by new leadership and spiritual regeneration. For while Carlyle was quite happy to advocate some fairly radical proposals to improve working-class conditions materially – including universal education and considerable emigration – ultimately such solutions would, he argued, be useless without overcoming the spiritual impoverishment that the market economy had brought about. Thus, in his later works, such as *On Heroes and Hero-Worship* (1841), *Past and Present* (1843) and the *Latter Day Pamphlets* (1850), Carlyle argued for a recovery of 'heroic' leadership, maintaining that heroism was one of the most serious casualties of instrumental thinking. In particular, in the economic sphere, he exhorted 'captains of industry' to show heroic leadership, so that they would, amongst other things, care for their employees properly. In doing so, Carlyle was not simply offering a hymn to the lost virtues of 'feudalism', since he was aware that the latter was a far from perfect system, and was in any case no longer possible after the Enlightenment had released its critical energies. But he was, nevertheless, seeking to revive pre-industrial values of loyalty and deference within an organic and hierarchically ordered society; without such a revival, he argued, mankind would be left spiritually crippled and inadequately governed (Francis and Morrow 1994: 166–71).

To some extent Carlyle's conservative vision looked back to the romantic critiques of the Enlightenment, such as Southey's, that we examined in Chapter 2. But although Carlyle's thought was in some ways typical of the earlier nineteenth century, it continued to have important echoes later in the Victorian period, as we can see if we briefly consider one of his spiritual successors, John Ruskin. Most famous for his work as an art critic, in such works as *Modern Painters* (1843–60) and *The Stones of Venice* (1851–3), Ruskin was also a virulent critic of liberal capitalism and the theory of political economy. Thus, like Carlyle, Ruskin criticized the excessive focus on material goods that he believed political economy had fostered, and, in *Unto This Last* (1862) in particular, attacked the assumptions he felt lay behind it. Key to his critique was that political economy encouraged the maximization of monetary accumulation at all costs, and hence led to greedy and selfish behaviour – whereas, he argued, 'the final outcome and consummation of all wealth is in the producing as many as possible full-breathed, bright-eyed, happy-hearted human creatures' (Ruskin 1903–12: XVII, 55–6). To achieve this, Ruskin argued, following Carlyle, society should be organized organically, to ensure that every individual has the opportunity to develop his capacities to the fullest extent, but also recognizing that there are profound inequalities between individuals – so that 'all forms of government are good just so far as they attain this one vital necessity of policy – *that the wise and kind, few or many, shall govern the unwise and unkind*' (Ruskin 1903–12: XVII, 236).

Some of the implications Ruskin took from this position were radical; for example, he argued that it justified government interference with existing property rights, since if property were either deemed to have been acquired through exploitation or deployed wastefully so that it did not contribute to maximizing human good, it might reasonably be redistributed. But many other implications were conservative, in particular Ruskin's strong defence of natural inequality and of a conception of government as being a 'rule of the best' with few institutional limitations. Since the duty of government was to maintain the organic nature of society and ensure just outcomes for the community, this left little room for a major focus on individual rights. The essential thing, as Ruskin himself bluntly put it, was that 'all creatures be made to do right; how they are made to it – by pleasant promises, or hard necessities, pathetic oratory, or the whip – is comparatively immaterial' (Bradley and Ousby 1987: 255).

If Carlyle and Ruskin were specifically concerned about the onset of modernity because of the effects of liberal capitalism and political economy on politics and society, other pessimistic conservative thinkers in this period were more worried about the impact that the advent of mass democracy as a whole might have on traditional structures and values. To some extent, their worries paralleled those of the 'ex-liberal' conservatives like Mallock and Spencer, described above – namely that in a mass democracy, states would be encouraged to tax income and property more extensively to fund nascent welfare states, in response to the demands of newly enfranchised working-class voters. This challenge remained important, of course, well into the twentieth century, as we shall see in the next chapter, with conservatives reacting to it in a variety of different ways after the First World War. But the concern of late nineteenth-century conservatives went deeper, since for them the onset of mass culture represented an irreversible decline, not something that could be managed simply by maintaining existing property rights or limiting state intervention. There were a number of such thinkers in this period, and indeed in the twentieth century, but one of the most notable was the American theorist Henry Adams. As we have seen, the most popular form of conservatism in the late nineteenth century in the USA was based around a strong commitment to liberal capitalism, articulated most forcefully by W. G. Sumner; nevertheless, there were still a number of prominent American conservative pessimists, including the literary critics Paul Elmer More and Irving Babbitt, as well as Adams's own brother Brooke. But Henry Adams was arguably the most important of all of them.

Henry Adams was the great-grandson of the second president, John Adams, and grandson of the sixth president, John Quincy Adams. He was as contemptuous of socialism as the followers of Sumner, but saw it as part of a much longer process of decay and degeneration in Western history. Fundamentally, Adams maintained, this was due to the gradual turning away of mankind from spiritual power (epitomized by the Virgin Mary) – whose zenith was the thirteenth century – to the ideal of physical power (epitomized by the image of 'the Dynamo'), a process that gradually transformed human society from one focused on wonder and beauty to one at the mercy of mechanical forces. The result was a situation in which man's own acquisition of scientific knowledge had been his undoing, so that what optimistic Enlightenment thinkers – and after them social evolutionary theorists – had facilely interpreted as 'progress' had in fact been a long process of decline by which human beings became increasingly subject to the very forces they themselves had unleashed. This process, according to Adams, could be observed beginning with the 'Mechanical Phase' of modern history, starting around 1600, and gathering speed with the 'Electric Phase' of mankind's development, which began around 1870, so that with the discovery of the nature of the element Radium in 1900, the results were clear. 'Power leaped from every atom ... Man could no longer hold it off. Force grasped his wrists and flung him about as though he had hold of a live wire or a runaway automobile', he declared (Adams 1918: 494–5).

But the future brought only even more depressing news. Impressed by the second law of thermodynamics, with its baleful conclusion that 'entropy increases', Adams predicted that the manic 'Electric Phase' would be succeeded in 1917 by the 'Ethereal Phase', where the molecule, the atom and the electron would be subjugated by thought – but only as a prelude to the degradation of energy entirely (Kirk 2008: 317). Politically too, this meant inevitable disaster. For if capitalism, with its myopic focus on increasing prosperity and maximizing material well-being, was deeply obnoxious – and which Adams explicitly linked, anti-Semitically, to the degradation of Christendom by the Jews – its replacement would be worse. The result of reducing humanity to mechanical economic forces meant that there was no conceptual defence to the replacement of capitalism by state socialism, Adams believed, since the demands of the mass of labourers would be impossible to resist. The warning signs were already there, he argued, citing as evidence the appearance of death duties, and the under-mining of silver as the basis of the currency by gold (Adams 1918: 501). But ultimately socialism would be succeeded by social rot, since the irresistible hold of scientific forces in modernity made this inevitable. If this was in some ways a blessing, since socialism was the very epitome of corruption and degradation, the replacement would be little better, since it would approximate to entropy reaching its height. The ultimate end would be eternal night and endless space for mankind, Adams maintained, such was the degree of his pessimism (Kirk 2008: 317).

Conclusion

What emerges from our examination of conservatism in this period, then, is how surprisingly effective conservatives were at dealing with the new challenges presented to them. One might have expected conservatives to find it difficult to come to terms with the globalization of the economy, increasing demands for social reform and the intensification of nationalism and imperialism, and certainly there were conservative thinkers, like Ruskin and Henry Adams, who lamented the effects of modernity. But as we have seen, there were also many others, like Cecil and Sumner, who adapted conservatism in order to colonize ideological spaces previously occupied by liberals, and conservative nationalists, like Barrès and Brunetière, who were able to harness changing intellectual fashions for conservative ends. In Chapter 4, we will move on to examine how conservatives sought to adapt to the advent of mass democracy, the rise of Soviet communism and the effects of two world wars.

4
Conservatism in the Era of the Two World Wars

New Challenges: From the First World War to the 1960s

In this chapter, we will examine how conservatism developed after the First World War, to the 1960s. In some ways the challenges that conservatives faced in the aftermath of the First World War, and even that of the Second, remained similar to those they had faced in the nineteenth century. As we saw in Chapter 3, conservatives had already been confronted with the multiple challenges of urbanization and industrialization, the increase in popularity of socialism, the expansion of state activity and the spectre of 'mass' politics – and these were challenges that remained as important, if not more so, in the twentieth century. Industrialization continued and intensified, particularly in countries where it had previously lagged behind (such as the USSR); more radical and interventionist governments were formed, particularly after the Depression of the 1930s in the USA as well as Europe; and electorates were fully enfranchised for the first time in Western democracies, notably in many cases giving women a full right to vote for the first time. But even when familiar problems recurred, they often did so in a significantly different way, and there were also entirely new developments for conservatives to respond to in this period of the twentieth century. Broadly speaking, conservatives faced three new challenges

First, although there were certain continuities that spanned the two world wars, both conflicts had significant and long-lasting consequences that fundamentally altered the nature of politics and the economy, particularly in Western Europe, but also in the USA. Economically, the First World War disrupted established global trade patterns, so that, to give just one example, Britain permanently lost a significant share of its overseas market for textiles to Japan and China (O'Rourke 2014: 82). The war also altered the global economic balance of power, since by the end of it both Britain and France were in considerable debt, whereas the USA had become the world's biggest creditor, its economy outperforming those of Britain and France in the 1920s by a considerable margin (Wardley 2011: 105). Politically, the First World War also had major direct effects, causing the collapse of the Ottoman, German, Austro-Hungarian and Russian empires; the redrawing of the global map, notably in Eastern Europe and the Middle East; and the establishment of a League of Nations that was supposed to prevent future disputes (Gerwarth 2017). But the indirect effects of the war were arguably just as significant, if not more so. Economically, given the new ascendancy of the USA and the punitive terms of the Treaty of Versailles (which demanded huge war reparations from the defeated Central Powers), Germany in particular, but other Western economies too, were particularly dependent on the continued economic success of the United States. If the Great Depression of the 1930s was not directly a result of the decisions made at the conclusion of the First World War – since they caused neither the intense market speculations in the USA in the 1920s, nor the protectionist responses by the American government to the dramatic Wall Street Crash in 1929 – nevertheless those decisions had made Western Europe peculiarly vulnerable to a slump in the US economy. Equally, if the legacy of the First World War did not make the rise of Nazism in Germany inevitable – since this would be to ignore other factors, including the lack of a genuine democracy in Germany before 1914 – there is no question that the humiliation Germany felt at the imposition of the Treaty of Versailles, and its economic dependence on the United States, made it a particularly fertile ground for the far Right in the early 1930s (Blinkhorn 2011: 321–2).

Turning to the Second World War, this also had significant direct and indirect consequences for society and politics, which conservatives necessarily had to respond to. Economically, the war again had major implications for the great powers, with Britain in particular ending up in considerable debt, particularly to the United States, while the latter again benefited, entering the post-war period as the globe's undisputed pre-eminent economic power. Partly because of this shift in economic pre-eminence, the Second World War also had important political consequences, with the previously hegemonic imperial powers, Britain and France, losing global influence to the USA and USSR (Hanhimaki 2014: 283–4). Domestically, and also as a consequence of the war, Western democracies tended to become more *collectivist* and more tolerant of state organization of society (Eley 2014). But again, it was perhaps the indirect effects of the Second World War that were most significant. Western governments became much more ready to intervene in the economy after 1945, partly as a result of the failure of economic reconstruction after the First World War, but also, more immediately, because of their experience of government intervention during the Second World War. Thus, not only did they set up a system of fixed exchange rates at Bretton Woods in 1944, to help reduce currency fluctuations, which lasted until 1970, they also became much more willing to countenance direct government intervention to stimulate demand, under the influence of the economist John Maynard Keynes (Crafts and Toniolo 2014: 374–6). Politically, the Second World War not only directly weakened the global influence of Britain and France, but also helped to crystallize the struggle for world supremacy between the USA and the USSR. And not only did the war lead to more collectivism in practice, it also led to an abiding belief among many intellectuals and policy-makers that the wartime state had been a model of efficiency, one that could be applied in peacetime to improve society. One of the most influential of such thinkers was Karl Mannheim, whose *Man and Society in an Age of Reconstruction* (1940) was a particular inspiration in the post-war period.

The second major challenge that conservatives faced in the middle of the twentieth century was the rise of various forms of socialism and communism. As we saw in the previous chapter, socialism, along with other kinds of progressive thought, had already developed significantly in the nineteenth century, producing a sophisticated body of political thought and inspiring important left-wing political parties in the years before the First World War, notably in Germany, and to a lesser extent in Britain. But it was the success of the Bolshevik Revolution in 1917, and the subsequent establishment of a Soviet state in Russia, that rendered the situation much more highly charged, not least because the USSR was officially committed to encouraging communist revolutions in other countries, through the Comintern, or Third Communist International (Chase 2011: 292). Given this background, reading Marx and other socialist thinkers became a much more controversial activity – even in Britain, where Marxist thought became more popular after the onset of the Depression in the 1930s, but especially in the United States, where just teaching Marx in a university could get academics into serious trouble during the era of McCarthyism (Susskind 2011).

Moreover, the challenge from the Left came not only from the communists. After the Depression, and certainly in the post-war period, social democratic parties in Britain and continental Europe, and Franklin Roosevelt's New Deal in the United States, posed a less dramatic but perhaps even more formidable threat to the conservative cause. Partly due to the collective experience of waging war, partly due to the hardships of the Depression, and partly due to a desire to halt the march of communism (by demonstrating that capitalist societies could look after their citizens better than communist ones), social democracy proved to be highly popular in the middle of the twentieth century, at least until the OPEC oil crisis in 1973 and the economic slowdown that followed in its wake.

Social democracy had a number of different variants, but, broadly speaking, it aimed to create greater equality in society, partly by direct redistribution of income through taxation, but more especially by the provision of comprehensive welfare services, which for the first time aimed to take care of citizens 'from the cradle to the grave'. Often, as in Anthony Crosland's influential book *The Future of Socialism* (1956), it was envisaged that such welfare states could be easily funded by increasing economic growth, an assumption that seemed plausible in the economic 'golden age' of the 1950s and 1960s, when Western economies generally achieved unprecedented growth rates compared to the interwar period, or even the nineteenth century. Such faith in the ability of governments to secure economic growth was often linked to a belief that economic planning could be used to guarantee this. This assumption was more plausible in an era of fixed exchange rates, which gave governments greater control over their national economies, even if there were divisions amongst social democrats over what kind of 'planning' was most efficacious.

Finally, conservatives in the mid-twentieth century had to adjust to an intellectual environment which, particularly after the Second World War, had become more sceptical of the worth of political ideologies and indeed to some extent of political ideas in general. Given that, as we saw in previous chapters, conservatives had often been deeply suspicious of progressive political ideologies, which they blamed for attempts at over-rapid social reconstruction that failed to respect the fallibility of human nature, this change in the intellectual environment was not necessarily to their disadvantage. But since the growing scepticism towards political ideologies had a number of quite different causes – some of which threatened ideals that conservatives themselves espoused, or provided support for political positions that were not conservative at all – the situation was not as comfortable for conservatives as might first appear.

Essentially, there were three distinct reasons why intellectuals became sceptical of political ideas at this point. Firstly, since espousing consistent political ideologies in the 1930s, whether on the Left or the Right, seemed to have led directly to utopian thinking, and ultimately to 'totalitarianism' – a concept much in vogue in the 1950s and 1960s – being wary of their use seemed like simple common sense. Indeed, because an over-rigid, over-rationalist adherence to political ideologies seemed a denial of the very limits of human reason, using them at all was, in the view of many post-war intellectuals, at best fraught with danger and at worst a pernicious form of self-deception. Such a view was, to pick just one example, common amongst the participants at the famous Congress for Cultural Freedom conference on the 'Future of Freedom', held in Milan in 1955 (Scott-Smith 2002).

Secondly, given the success of post-war politicians and policy-makers in achieving historically high rates of economic growth, and in establishing welfare states that were much more generous than previously, there seemed much less reason to debate the worth of competing political ideologies – not least because such successes were often attributed to the new-found technical skill of economists and political scientists, rather than to adhering to any given political ideology (Bell 2000; Lipset 1960: 4).

Lastly, on a more theoretical level, the worth of political ideas of all kinds came under fire in the post-war era from the intellectual movement known as positivism – premised on the belief that the only genuine way of gaining true knowledge, including in the humanities, was through the application of scientific method. This took two main forms. In the first place, there were behaviourist political scientists – particularly in the United States, such as David Easton and Harold Lasswell – who argued bluntly that human behaviour could be explained on a purely causal basis, and that as such analysing political ideas and ideologies was largely a waste of time, since it did not get to the root of what genuinely motivated human beings (Easton 1953; Lasswell and Kaplan 1950). Secondly, there were linguistic positivists, like the British philosopher T. D. Weldon, for whom the only statements that could be meaningful were those that were self-evidently true – such as '2+2=4' – or those that were empirically testable. Since value-laden statements could never pass such a test, Weldon argued, there could be no legitimate place for normative political arguments, let alone political ideologies. Political principles ultimately came down to the prejudices or emotions of political philosophers (or politicians), hence, necessarily, they could have no cognitive status. In short, according to Weldon, since there was no legitimate way of testing normative political arguments, no rational means of advocating them was possible (Weldon 1953: 13–15; Neill 2013).

Conservative Response I: Embracing Mass Democracy – Stanley Baldwin and Michael Oakeshott

Broadly speaking, conservatives produced four main ideological responses to these new challenges. First, some conservatives, particularly in Britain, sought to minimize the damage to nineteenth-century traditions done by the two world wars, and to negotiate the shift to mass democracy, by relying on traditional methods – namely, distorting the ideological positions of their opponents, and seeking to manage change incrementally. Good examples of this can be found in the writings of Stanley Baldwin, who as Conservative prime minister was the dominant political figure of the interwar period in Britain, and – on a more abstract level – in the work of the conservative political theorist and famous critic of post-war planning Michael Oakeshott.

For Baldwin, the key task was to re-establish social and political order in Britain after the trauma of the First World War, while minimizing the threat posed by the Labour Party, soon to be the main challenger to conservative hegemony after the passing of (near) universal suffrage in 1918 in Britain. To do this, Baldwin adopted two main strategies. More negatively, he sought to represent the Labour Party's socialism as foreign and mechanical, inimical to the great traditions of religion and common sense in Britain, and tainted with Russian Bolshevism, or at least with implausible rationalism. Thus, in the 1930s in particular, after the Labour Party began advocating emergency powers, nationalization and government planning more aggressively, Baldwin linked this to the growth of authoritarianism abroad – including Stalin's Russia, Hitler's Germany and even Franklin Roosevelt's New Deal – contrasting this with his own (conservative) version of British democracy. To quote Baldwin himself in 1934: 'this country today [is] the last stronghold of freedom, standing like a rock in a tide that is threatened to submerge the world' (Williamson 2003: 186). More positively, Baldwin sought to reconcile the advent of democracy with past tradition, arguing that although a democratic system of government was fraught with danger, requiring a most delicate balance – since it could easily tip into either anarchy or tyranny – it was also the logical culmination of English tradition (Williamson 2003: 190–1).[1] Through a slow and careful evolution of its historic institutions, in other words, by which a 'precious' conception of freedom had been developed and transmitted, England had proved itself ready to accommodate mass democracy. However, such an accommodation was not automatic, Baldwin believed – it required active cultivation, to ensure the disparate forces of modernity did not cause instability, as they had so ruinously during the First World War (Baldwin 1923; Williamson 2003: 191).

To do this, Baldwin set out to accomplish three objectives. In the first place, he sought to overcome divisions between country and town, waxing lyrically about the English countryside and rural life, but not at the expense of appreciating the importance of modern industry. Baldwin was, after all, born the son of a steel manufacturer, in stark contrast to the backgrounds of most previous Conservative prime ministers, and he made much of the fact that he was 'the only one of my colleagues who has lived for years under the smoke of factory chimneys' (Baldwin 1926: 6–7; Williamson 2003: 192). Secondly, Baldwin sought to uphold a form of Christianity that was inclusive and non-doctrinaire, aimed at overcoming sectarianism whilst upholding the Anglican establishment. Thus, far more than pre-1914 Conservative leaders, Baldwin sought to include Nonconformists in his version of Christianity, seeking their aid in opposing class divisions and materialism at home, and the 'paganism' and barbarism of Nazism and communism abroad (Baldwin 1926: 195–7, 202–11; Williamson 2003: 200). Finally, Baldwin attempted to downplay the aggressive imperialism of the Edwardian Conservative Party, and instead stressed the importance of a shared 'Englishness' and national character that would include all citizens. If such a conception had its exclusive function – in rejecting foreign socialism, rootless cosmopolitan intellectuals and misleading political rhetoric, in the manner of nineteenth-century conservatives – it also offered a principle to unite all classes, working men included. Key to Baldwin's conception was that the Labour movement should not be regarded as an enemy; rather, properly understood, it was a fine manifestation of the English spirit, containing 'many men ... who hold sane and just views of the possibilities of human progress ... with whom [Conservatives] may be able to work hand in hand to effect great improvements in the condition of our people' (Williamson 2003: 194). As such, even trade unions, often the subject of Conservative suspicion, could be used for positive purposes: there was no natural reason why employer and employed could not co-operate if they exercised appropriate goodwill, trust and understanding (Baldwin 1926: 33–4). For Baldwin, in short, despite the challenges posed by mass democracy, it was entirely possible for conservatism to flourish: if beneficent change needed careful fostering, then the traditional institutions England had gradually acquired offered every opportunity for success.

This strategy proved highly effective for conservatives in Britain seeking to come to terms with mass democracy in the period from 1918 to the 1960s. It is of course true that Baldwin's strategy had to be revised somewhat after the Second World War, given the widespread acceptance of much greater state intervention after the war, and the popularity of the welfare state enacted by the Attlee government of 1945–51, as described above. Nevertheless, conservatives in the 1950s found ways of continuing to appeal to a post-war mass electorate, by accepting the inevitability (or even desirability) of the welfare state, whilst emphasizing the new possibilities opening up as a result of rising affluence – very much a feature of that decade – as well as decrying the joylessness of their socialist opponents, whom they claimed were less reliable stewards of economic growth (Jarvis 2005; Black 2003). In parallel, such strategies also found favour in the United States, where, following the lead of Sumner, Republicans in the 1920s had sought to recommend the possibilities of mass capitalism to a much wider number of citizens – combined with a firm commitment to isolationism after the Americans' intervention in the First World War. (Not for nothing did President Calvin Coolidge declare in 1925 that 'the chief business of the American people is business', upholding what had become by the 1920s a virtual truism.) Despite the souring of this vision in the 1930s – after the failure of the US banking system to cope with the Wall

Street Crash of 1929 and the resulting Depression, and the acceptance of much greater state intervention with the New Deal in the 1930s and 1940s – a revised version of conservative capitalism under the presidency of Dwight Eisenhower in the 1950s proved both possible and popular. As in Britain, this version of conservative capitalism gave a certain amount of ground to social democracy – though in the USA less GDP was spent on welfare, and no socialist party appeared – but if anything it embraced affluence even more strongly, riding an unprecedently high rate of economic growth, and encouraging a huge increase in property ownership.

If Baldwin offered strategies for conservatives to respond to the challenge of mass democracy on a practical level, the political philosopher Michael Oakeshott put forward arguments for conservatives seeking to come to terms with democracy and modernity on a more abstract level. To do this, Oakeshott sought to *base* his commitment to modernist conceptions of individual liberty and pluralism on conservative arguments about tradition and historical change, essentially justifying his position with reference to three key points.

First, in various essays in *Rationalism in Politics and Other Essays* (1962), Oakeshott famously argued that no activities, including political ones, could be performed without *practical* as well as *technical* knowledge. By 'practical' he meant the kind of knowledge that cannot be precisely formulated, that resists reduction to 'rules, principles, directions [and] maxims', and instead 'exists only in use, is not reflective' and 'can neither be taught nor learned, but only imparted and acquired' (Oakeshott 1991: 12). On this basis, he claimed, it followed that the correct approach to political activity was to rely on tradition, on inherited practical knowledge, eschewing radical innovation and reliance on abstract political ideologies, which necessarily fail to respect the importance of practical knowledge (Neill 2010: 41–2).[2] Second, however, Oakeshott also believed that one of the great achievements bequeathed to us by the Western tradition is the gradual emergence of a modern conception of individuality – of the idea that individuals' being able to pursue their different life-plans constitutes a vital component of their happiness. Genuinely celebrating such an achievement,

Oakeshott argued, meant fully embracing modern pluralism, refusing to lament the loss of the communal institutions of the medieval and early modern eras, or (worse) trying to recreate such communal ties in modernity by appealing to concepts that fail to respect pluralism, such as 'community' or 'the public good' (Oakeshott 1975: 81, 54; 1991: 366–8; Neill 2010: 59–61).[3] Third, therefore, in *On Human Conduct* (1975) Oakeshott advocated a form of government that could best respect such modern pluralism, namely 'civil association', which is based upon the idea that laws should be impersonal, enabling citizens to pursue their individual ends, without prescribing an end for the state as a whole. Such a system of laws, Oakeshott conceded, would always be to some extent an abstraction, lacking the flexibility of practical moral response; nevertheless, it represented the best attempt at a system of government that respected individual differences, and as such was the type of state which commanded the most genuine authority (Oakeshott 1975: 124–30; Neill 2010: 61–9; 2015: 49–51). In short, Oakeshott's conception of the state was genuinely conservative in that its legitimacy ultimately rested on the authority of tradition; equally, however, it embraced modernity, or at least aspects of it, and maintained that modern mass democracies were at least potentially capable of respecting individualism (Neill 2017).

Conservative Response II: Elitist Sociology – Vilfredo Pareto

Some conservatives, then, particularly in Britain and the USA, sought to respond to the challenges of mass democracy by finding ways to accommodate it, cautiously recommending its possibilities of increased liberty and prosperity, whilst downplaying the plausibility of socialism to the public. A second group, however, took a more cynical view of the onset of mass democracy, and in particular of the idea that in the era of the masses governments could ever really 'represent' the interests of people in general. In view of this, such thinkers looked for ways to justify the continued rule of elites, often using information gleaned from the new discipline of sociology – which, as we saw in Chapter 3, had already developed systematically in the late nineteenth and early twentieth centuries. A good example of such a thinker – though far from the only one – was the Italian economist and sociologist Vilfredo Pareto.

Pareto, like Oakeshott, dismissed notions such as 'the common good' or 'the general will' on the basis that these were illegitimate, bogus concepts which claimed to be rational aims for the collective, when in fact their appeal was actually emotional, not rational. (On this basis, in such works as *Socialist Systems* [1902], Pareto rejected socialism as an ideology, since he believed such concepts to be intrinsic to it.) But he went further than Oakeshott in dismissing the very possibility of representation itself, rejecting the idea that the state – however imperfectly – could produce rules related to the moral convictions of the public. Rather, in his *Treatise of General Sociology* (1916), Pareto maintained that humans are always ultimately motivated by emotions, or 'emotional residues', and hence are always vulnerable to various types of strategic persuasion. The real question, therefore, was how different types of elite could manage to maintain power; following Machiavelli's famous distinction, Pareto divided these types into 'foxes' and 'lions'. 'Foxes' preferred to be cunning, to try to rule by (manipulated) consent; 'lions' were more inclined to employ force (Pareto 1916: paras 889, 888). Critically though, Pareto argued, both types of political elite have to maintain power by recruiting support from much more diverse social and economic groups, distinguishing in particular between innovative 'speculators' on the one hand, and more cautious investing 'rentiers' on the other.

According to Pareto, this leads to an inevitable 'circulation' of elites corresponding to different socio-economic cycles. Initially, 'foxes' tend to seduce speculators to their cause by helping them openly or clandestinely despoil the rentiers, encouraging rising prosperity and a consumer boom, which also leads to the questioning of traditional norms. However, eventually the boom would sour due to over-consumption based upon credit, while conversely a lack of available capital and of productive investment would lead to a contraction of the economy. The necessity for restraint and saving of capital would therefore become apparent, and the result was inevitably a more conservative government, comprised of 'lions', and backed by the rentiers. In time, however, the people would tire of such austerity, causing the start of a new cycle (Pareto 1916: paras 2053–9, 2223–36). The onset of parliamentary democracy tended to encourage 'foxish' tendencies, whereby politicians worked to establish clientelistic networks of speculators, Pareto maintained, but equally this was liable to produce an authoritarian reaction. Pareto therefore greeted the appearance of the fascist regime of Benito Mussolini in 1922 as confirming 'splendidly the predictions of my *Sociology* and many of my articles' (Bellamy 2003: 90). However, Pareto was not personally a fascist, and his theory did not endorse fascism. If he departed from previous conservatives in having a more cynical view of traditions and traditional elites, his theory remained ultimately a conservative one: his sociology was harnessed to the goal of managing change cautiously; he regarded individuals as subject to 'extra-human' socio-economic tendencies; and he was determinedly elitist.

Conservative Response III: Values from the Ancient World – Leo Strauss

Thus far, we have examined two types of conservatives who sought to come to terms with mass democracy in the twentieth century, the second much more cynically than the first. The third type of conservative reacted more stridently to what they saw as the problems of modernity, appealing to the past standards of tradition in order to criticize modern life. Such conservatives tended to be particularly critical of the failure of mass democracies to respect traditional values, and, as such, were often even more critical of what they saw as the 'value-free' nature of liberalism than they were of socialism. To some extent, therefore, they resembled the pessimistic conservatives of the later nineteenth century, such as Ruskin, Carlyle and Henry Adams, but if anything they were even more radical. Confronted with the reality of mass democracy

– as opposed to its looming arrival – and deeply disturbed by the positivist distinction between fact and value in ethical and political theory, such conservatives sought to appeal to absolute standards from the past in order to reform present society. There are a number of proponents of this approach that we could consider, but we will concentrate here on arguably the most radical and influential of them, namely the German American émigré political philosopher Leo Strauss.

In Strauss we encounter a thinker who considered the problems of mass societies to be very deep-seated. Although he was undoubtedly critical of what he viewed as the morally neutral nature of modern Western democracies, and of the technocratic and positivist political theory that he saw as symbiotically linked to this pathological state, for him these problems ultimately lay in the way that modernity itself had developed. According to Strauss, in modernity the norms of classical natural right had gradually been undermined, so that objective standards of right and wrong had been devalued. This, he maintained, had occurred in three stages, which he delineated in particular in *Natural Right and History* (1953).

First, Machiavelli and Hobbes had fundamentally lowered the standards of moral conduct. Machiavelli stressed the importance of following objectives that could be attained in the real world, rather than aiming for the very best state, as Plato had done; while Hobbes exacerbated this, privileging the importance of self-preservation above a genuine standard of good (Strauss 1975: 40–1, 49; 1953: 166–202). This position was then adapted somewhat by Locke to stress the importance of property to a much greater degree, but this did not alter the fundamental change that had already occurred – that mankind had shifted from asking questions about the nature of virtue to ones about maximizing material well-being and why we should obey the law (Strauss 1975: 50; 1953: 202–51). The situation was made worse by the second stage of modernity, which was initiated by Rousseau. Rousseau attempted to return to classical standards, to the world of the ancient Greek polis, by advocating loyalty to the city-state through the mechanism of the 'General Will', but instead of solving the problem, he just intensified it. For if in the thought of Hobbes and Locke there was still the possibility of an appeal to a higher law, in Rousseau's thought

(Strauss argued) this was ruled out – instead the 'General Will' becomes the highest moral law; the highest moral values of mankind thus become subject to human will and hence (by extension) to historical vicissitudes. This conclusion was underlined by the work of Hegel, who claimed that history itself constituted a process by which human values were optimized (Strauss 1975: 51–6). Finally, the last stage of this process was inaugurated by Nietzsche, who confronted the fact that history did not provide any real evidence of human progress, and concluded that, as such, values were simply the creation of human will or power. Although any attempt to apply Nietzsche politically was a perversion of his doctrines, Strauss conceded, nevertheless Nietzsche's thought provided little resistance to those advocating fascism who *did* seek to apply his doctrines (Strauss 1975: 94–7).

From this radical critique of modernity Strauss drew emphatically conservative conclusions. First, although he thought that modern liberalism was deeply damaging, because it necessarily implies radical relativism under the guise of 'tolerance', Strauss maintained some hope that a proper theory of liberal democracy, or 'classical liberalism', could be saved by the application – or 'recollection' – of the theories of natural right. This was because, Strauss claimed, 'the theory of liberal democracy ... originated in the first and second waves of modernity', and thus derived powerful support from pre-modern modes of thought (Strauss 1975: 98). If recreating the politics of the ancient world was no longer feasible, therefore, it was nevertheless possible to relearn certain ancient truths – not least the vital importance of virtue for the health of a political system. Thus, while modern liberalism was certainly in crisis, it could be saved by the judicious application of past knowledge and the conservative strategy of controlling change (Strauss 1964: 1, 11–12).

From this Strauss drew two further conclusions. First, modern citizens needed to re-establish, conceptually, that although there is a universal valid hierarchy of ends, there are no universally valid rules for action (Strauss 1953: 162). (Notoriously, however, Strauss believed that it may well be necessary to pretend to ordinary citizens that the rules of the state *are* immutable – in other words to lie to them – in order to ensure their obedience to those laws.) Second, it was vital to promote the right kind of education to rectify the failures of modern liberalism. The latter, Strauss argued, crucially refused to admit that there are fixed norms, preferring to respond to changing needs, and was by nature optimistic and radical, favouring the application of technological solutions rather than learning about moral choices.[4] In response, Strauss argued that 'true liberals today have no more pressing duty than to counteract the perverted liberalism which contends that just to live, securely and happily ... is man's simple but supreme goal', and advocated an education that reminded human beings of the vital importance of quality, excellence and virtue (Strauss 1968: 64). And if Strauss was clear that only some individuals were capable of benefiting from this education – since the ability of humans to achieve moral excellence was not, by nature, equal – then, if anything, this made it all the more vital to institute such an education.

Conservative Response IV: Values from Christianity – T. S. Eliot and Jacques Maritain

If Strauss sought to criticize the nature of modern liberalism by appealing (in qualified fashion) to the standards of ancient philosophy, a fourth group of conservatives in this period sought to do so by appealing to the values of Christianity instead. Like Strauss, these conservatives were concerned by the potential for mass democracies to become 'rootless' and amoral, a concern that was only heightened by the advent of fascism and Bolshevism. Thus they, like Strauss, were deeply sceptical of the worth of liberal 'tolerance', behind which they felt lurked a pernicious 'neutrality' or even outright relativism, and argued that the only alternative was a commitment to more absolute moral standards. But however ambivalent such conservatives were about the advent of modernity, and apprehensive of the effects of mass democracy, they were nevertheless more optimistic than Strauss that universal human values could be protected in a democracy – and certainly without actually lying to the populace. To explore this type of conservatism, we will briefly examine two prominent proponents of it, namely the distinguished Anglo-American poet and cultural conservative T. S. Eliot, and the influential French Catholic thinker Jacques Maritain.

Taking T. S. Eliot first, what characterized his work was an insistence that a particular conception of 'culture' was vital for the continued health of modern democracies, and that Christianity formed a vital component of such a culture. Eliot's arguments evolved somewhat from the 1930s to the post-war period, from *The Idea of a Christian Society* (1939) to *Notes Towards the Definition of Culture* (1948). In the former, Eliot argued for a demanding Christian ideal; in the latter he cast his arguments in more pragmatic and socio-logical terms. Nevertheless, in both works his position rested on three fundamental tenets.

First, Eliot believed that an elite was necessary to maintain a national culture, and that such an elite should be composed of a 'Community of Christians' who practised their religion particularly thoughtfully and self-consciously, and who were distinguished from the largely unreflective 'Christian Community' of the wider society. To some extent this conception was reminiscent of Coleridge's earlier 'clerisy', but crucially Eliot (unlike Coleridge) did not seek to identify those suitable for this elite by their vocations. Instead, he argued more vaguely that it should be composed of members of the clergy and laity who were 'more conscious [and] more intellectually developed' and who shared 'a common system of education and a common culture', at most increasingly hinting in the *Notes* that this group would most likely be found in sections of the educated upper middle class in the twentieth century, rather than the aristocracy (Eliot 1939: 42, 40, 35, 37).

Second, Eliot maintained that a properly functioning elite could not be achieved through the operation of a classless 'meritocracy' – an increasingly popular idea in the aftermath of the Second World War – since this would not guarantee the survival of hard-won traditional cultural values. Instead, in a manner somewhat akin to Burke, he argued that such values could only be sustained across generations if they were transmitted in a more evolutionary manner by the elite, and that as such the elite would have to be drawn chiefly 'from the dominant class of the time', since they were 'the primary consumers of the work of thought and art' (Eliot 1948: 42). While Eliot conceded that a flourishing (Christian) culture also depended on a certain diversity and even 'friction' within it, in a way that sounded almost like Mill at times, it should be stressed that such diversity was ultimately (and importantly) to be limited by the framework of tradition. Thus for Eliot, quite as much as for Oakeshott, the 'diversity' being upheld was stressed largely in polemical opposition to the uniformity threatened by the onset of post-war planning and the popularity of 'rationalism in politics', rather than primarily being aimed against the potentially deadening effects of outdated traditions (Eliot 1948: 58, 44; Collini 2000: 223).

Finally, although he was undoubtedly deeply conservative, this did not preclude Eliot from making some sharp criticisms of capitalism, particularly in his earlier work. Thus in *The Idea of a Christian Society*, he claimed that an obsession with private profit and 'unregulated industrialism' had led to a situation where it was unclear that British society was based around anything more permanent 'than a belief in compound interest and the maintenance of dividends' (Eliot 1939: 64). As such, although the main thrust of Eliot's work was clearly to assert the continuing importance of a traditional cultural elite, this did not prevent him from advocating changes to the organization of modern industry and commerce, quite as much as his nineteenth-century predecessors, the cultural conservatives Ruskin and Carlyle.

If for Eliot Christianity was vitally important because it formed an irreplaceable part of a flourishing culture, for other conservatives, particularly after the Second World War, it was crucial because it provided a basis on which to assert the fundamental dignity of human individuals. This assertion arose largely due to the new intellectual and political challenges described earlier – namely the positivistic tendency to minimize the extent to which human values could be rationally grounded, and, more brutally, the continuing existence of totalitarian regimes that did not respect the worth of individuals at all. As such, assertions of the fundamental importance of valuing individuals were hardly unique to conservatives: representatives of other ideological families, notably liberals, sought to give this doctrine reality by embedding a commitment to universal human rights in such post-war organizations as the European Court of Human Rights and the United Nations. But clearly conservatives had to meet this challenge too, and for them positivism (in its various forms) posed particular problems. For if conservatives could afford to be fairly insouciant about the idea that political ideologies could not be rationally justified – since that chimed with their own dismissal of ideologies as 'abstract' and 'rationalist' – the problem remained that positivism also tended to undermine the idea that traditions should be valued for their own sake – an implication much more damaging for their ideology. Hence the attraction for some conservatives, particularly in continental Europe, of Catholic Christianity, since this provided an absolute foundation for their beliefs at a time when political ideas of all types were being questioned hard. One of the most sophisticated of such conservatives was the French thinker Jacques Maritain, who played an influential role in trying to reconcile Catholicism and democracy in continental Europe, particularly after the Second World War.

Maritain's thought had three key features. First, he argued that democracy was not merely compatible with Christianity, but in fact the logical *implication* of it. Thus, in a 1942 pamphlet, he claimed that 'democracy is linked to Christianity and ... the democratic impulse has arisen in human history as the moral manifestation of the inspiration of the Gospel', even declaring that 'democracy is the only way of bringing about a moral rationalization of politics' (Maritain 1950a: 37; Muller 2013a: 136). This represented a stark contrast to the wariness the Catholic Church had tended to show towards the initial development of democracy in the nineteenth century – even to the extent of being ambivalent about explicitly Catholic parties – on the grounds that the universality of Catholicism should not be confused with the pluralism intrinsic to democracy. Second, however, Maritain conversely argued that modern democracies required Catholic Christianity in order to flourish. This was because, he maintained, only Catholicism could provide proper guidance on the goals individuals should aim at, through the doctrines of natural law. By contrast, liberalism and communism alike were unable to provide such guidance, and hence tended to degenerate into materialism. The USA, where Maritain fled the Nazis, was, he thought, a case in point: whilst its people had a generous, humanist spirit, the structures of its industrial capitalism lacked soul (Maritain 1958). In short, if Maritain was an important defender of universal human rights in the post-war era, even helping to draw up the United Nations Declaration of Human Rights, this defence was ultimately premised on a belief in natural rights derived from Catholic teaching.

Did such arguments mark out Maritain as a conservative? Arguably on their own they did not, since although conservatives certainly did take a belief in 'natural rights' as a basis for valuing traditional structures in society, other thinkers, including Catholic ones in this period, derived much more Left-leaning conclusions from that belief. Thus in the early post-war period, thinkers such as the Italian political theorist Giuseppe Dossetti and the French politician Georges Bidault argued that because Catholic theories of natural right emphasized the importance of community and solidarity, they justified substantial intervention in the free market and a generous welfare state (Muller 2013a: 138–40). The third feature of Maritain's thought, however, definitely *did* confirm him as a conservative, since his arguments retained elements of reactionary Catholic thought from the nineteenth century. In particular, in a manner reminiscent of Maistre and Bonald, he criticized Rousseau (and before him Protestants like Luther) for propagating the false idea of popular sovereignty, whereby the voluntary decisions of isolated individuals gave the state its legitimacy. Such a position was fundamentally mistaken, Maritain believed, since it mistook 'sovereignty' for a secular concept which could be located in the nation-state. Instead, he argued, because 'sovereignty' necessarily implied something 'separate' and 'transcendent', it could only properly refer to God himself, and thus the whole task of modern political theory was to regain a proper understanding of human beings' relationship to the divine. If Maritain departed from the earlier French reactionary thinkers in rejecting an overtly theocratic state, he nevertheless believed that his version of Christian democracy must ultimately be founded 'on the same principles (analogically speaking) as that of the Middle Ages' (Maritain 1950b: 343–4; Muller 2013a: 136–7). Notwithstanding his greater openness to democratic pluralism and individual rights, therefore, at bottom Maritain remained a deeply conservative Catholic thinker.

Conservatism and Fascism

These then, were the four main types of conservatism that appeared in the middle of the twentieth century, and in the final chapter we will examine how conservatives responded to the challenges that arose from the 1960s onwards. Before doing so, however, we need to address one final important question that inevitably arises when considering conservatism in this period – namely how to conceptualize the relationship between conservatism and fascism. Superficially, fascism appears to share a number of features with at least certain types of conservatism, in particular the advocacy of nationalism and rejection of liberal individualism, and the stress on 'natural' institutions such as the family and the nation over abstract ones such as economic equality and universal human rights. For this reason, a number of the thinkers we have examined, such as Maurice Barrès, Ferdinand Brunetière and Heinrich von Treitschke, and some we have not had time to look at, such as the influential right-wing French thinker Charles Maurras (1868–1952) and the German theorist Carl Schmitt (1888–1985), have been labelled as both 'conservative' and 'fascist'. As we have seen, the complexity of political ideologies means that it can be difficult to classify thinkers precisely – conservatism has sometimes overlapped significantly with both liberalism and socialism. Nevertheless, such was the importance of fascism as a phenomenon in the first half of the twentieth century that we should, however briefly, attempt to distinguish it from conservatism.

How, then, should fascism be defined and what distinguishes it from conservatism precisely? These questions are difficult to answer, since fascism lacks the precision of more developed ideologies like liberalism, socialism or conservatism, and indeed some fascists repudiated the very idea that it should be viewed as a consistent set of ideas at all. In view of this, some analysts of fascism such as Geoff Eley have even sought to analyse it as a socio-economic phenomenon, largely to be explained by the peculiar political circumstances after the First World War and the economic consequences of the 1930s Depression, rather than as a movement that had a fundamental ideological component (Eley 1983). Furthermore, fascism in practice took varying forms, and to some extent prioritized different goals – so that Mussolini's Italian variant tended to have more forward-looking, authoritarian nationalist impulses, while Hitler's 'national socialist' version tended to be more overtly racist, seeking to maintain or obtain racial purity, harking back to the glories of the German past. For these reasons, even when analysts have agreed that there is an inescapable ideological element to fascism, there have still been some sharp divisions between them – notably over the degree to which fascism should be understood as part of a late nineteenth-century historicist rebellion against the more rationalist elements of the Enlightenment (as Zeev Sternhall has notably argued) or as a more immediate response to the First World War (Sternhall 2001). However, despite these difficulties, it is arguably still possible to identify fascism's core principles, and hence to determine how closely it is related to conservatism. Essentially, fascism has four key facets, two of which are (sometimes) compatible with conservatism, and two of which are definitely not.

First, fascists strongly argue for nationalism against the progressive ideologies' espousal of internationalism, and like conservatives they sometimes link nationalism strongly with an ethnic or even biological identity (although not necessarily, since they may advocate nationalism on purely cultural grounds). If there is arguably a stronger tendency within fascism to argue for territorial expansion as a logical consequence of nationalism, this is not (as we have seen) something that conservatives necessarily rule out. Second, like conservatives, fascists have an ambivalent relationship with capitalism, sometimes favouring it (particularly when contrasting their position with socialist demands for equality), but also criticizing it for encouraging individualism and instrumentalism rather than promoting the national good. Third, however, on balance fascism tends to be more critical of capitalism than conservatives are. Such is the alienating effect of capitalism that (fascists believe) it cannot easily be reconciled with loyalty to the nation. Finally, following on from this point, fascists are necessarily more radical than conservatives. As we have seen, conservatives (such as, for example, W. H. Mallock) are sometimes happy to favour new classes over older ones, but this is always harnessed to the aim of managing change carefully and cautiously. By contrast, fascists are necessarily committed to producing an entirely new political culture, always through popular mobilization and often by violence, even if their aims are (partially) conceptualized in terms of returning to a glorious past, as well as a glorious future. Indeed, one can go further and suggest that increased radicalization and continued violence are inherent in the very structure of fascism, given the considerable tensions within its ideology. If fascists share some of the ideological terrain of conservatives, therefore, they are very far from being identical (Eatwell 1996).

Conclusion

In conclusion, then, conservatives in this era developed a wide range of responses to deal with the effects of the world wars, the rise of mass democracy and the challenge of various types of socialism. As we have seen, some conservatives sought to embrace modern democracies – though with mixed degrees of enthusiasm. Thus Oakeshott, albeit with caveats, thought that modernity genuinely offered individuals unprecedented opportunities to obtain freedom, whereas elitists like Pareto thought that mass democracies should be accepted because it would still be quite possible for elites to control them. By contrast, other conservatives, echoing the fears of earlier thinkers in the nineteenth century, argued that mass democracy could only be sustained by appealing to various kinds of absolute values, whether those of ancient philosophy (like Strauss) or Christianity (like Eliot and

Maritain). Despite challenging circumstances, then, conservatism proved to be highly adaptable in an era which many had predicted might be its undoing, in view of the disappearance of traditional elites. In the final chapter, we examine the rise of the New Right, and the opportunities and problems this created for conservatives.

5
Conservatism from the 1960s to the Present

New Challenges: From Permissiveness to Populism

In this chapter we will trace the development of conservatism from the 1960s to the present. To some extent, the challenges conservatives faced from the 1960s onwards resembled those in the early twentieth century. In particular, until the Velvet Revolution in 1989, and the formal end of the Soviet Union in 1991, opposition to communism remained key to almost all conservative positions, and, more widely, conservatives often continued to wrestle with the long-standing challenge of combining a commitment to traditional social values with promoting greater economic prosperity. Furthermore, even when they changed, some conservatives' positions evolved slowly; for example, in the 1980s and 1990s Christian democrats in many European countries continued to espouse positions largely familiar from the more immediate post-war era, as did various types of 'paternalist' or 'One Nation' conservatives in Britain, who took inspiration from Harold Macmillan, and before him Stanley Baldwin. However, such continuities should not be exaggerated, because conservatives also had to respond to a new set of social and economic conditions. Three in particular were especially significant.

First, most significantly, the economic environment in Western Europe and the United States fundamentally altered in the 1970s and 1980s. The single most important cause of this was the massive rise in oil prices that occurred in 1973 as a result of the leading oil-producing countries (OPEC) imposing an embargo against those that had supported Israel in the 1973 Arab–Israeli war. This had far-reaching consequences, particularly as this first oil 'shock' was exacerbated by a second significant rise in the price of oil in 1979, causing oil prices to increase overall by a factor of ten between 1973 and 1980. The result was a sharp end to the post-war economic 'golden age' that had existed since around 1951, with the twelve most advanced European economies seeing their economic growth decline from 4.8 per cent between 1960 and 1973 to 0.5 per cent during the first half of the 1980s. As a consequence of this, unemployment rose sharply in most Western economies, increasing tenfold in West Germany, for example, and remained high throughout the entire 1980s, at between 5 and 12 per cent. Inflation, too, partly as a result of the oil price rise, increased significantly, ballooning to an average of 10 per cent a year in Western Europe in the 1970s and 1980s; in Mediterranean Europe the rate was 20 per cent (Berend 2014: 407).

Second, these developments caused some of the fundamental assumptions about post-war economic policy to be thrown into question. In the first place, a more difficult economic landscape put considerable strain on the universal welfare states that had been developed in the aftermath of the Depression and the Second World War – and which had often significantly been expanded in the 1960s.[1] Already under increasing strain because more people were living longer (partly due to the very success of improved healthcare services), the reduction in economic growth in the 1970s meant that there was significantly less to spend on welfare – at the very moment more needed to be spent on unemployment benefit. In the second place, a tougher economic environment exacerbated the already existing trend away from heavy industries to services, as Western economies faced increasing competition from emerging economies like Japan and Taiwan, and the electronic revolution in any case totally transformed both what advanced economies produced and the way in which they operated (Singer 1998: 76, 77; Eichengreen 2007: 6–7). This in turn brought into question the wisdom of governments continuing to support heavy nationalized industries. For where previously there had been reasonable justifications for why governments should support these – namely that private companies had often failed to invest sufficiently, and governments could use their stake in such companies to plan their economies effectively – such justifications had become increasingly implausible, given the increasing switch to service industries and the more unpredictable nature of the global economy (Hannah 2004).

Finally, Keynesianism, the underlying theory that supported most of the economic assumptions of the post-war period, was also thrown into question. This was so above all because unemployment and inflation rose *at the same time* in the 1970s, in defiance of Keynesian arguments. Keynes had argued that unemployment was fundamentally caused by lack of demand, and that this could be solved by government spending money on public projects to stimulate it – albeit that this came with the potential danger of inflation. As such, by the 1970s, economists and public policy-makers alike had elevated the inverse relationship between unemployment and inflation to the status of dogma, embodied in the so-called 'Phillips curve', and its contradiction in practice came as a nasty shock (Maddison 1995: 84). Coupled with the United States' decision to end the Bretton Woods agreement in 1971, which rendered relationships between different currencies much more volatile, and hence reduced national governments' economic power, policy-makers were faced with the uncomfortable fact that Keynesian theories no longer seemed to provide authoritative advice for all circumstances, as they had in previous post-war decades (Berend 2014: 408).

The final change to which conservatives had to adapt in this period was a significant generational shift in social norms in many Western societies, which challenged many traditional forms of authority. Unlike their parents, many baby boomers began to question institutions that had previously been taken for granted – including the patriarchal family, traditional religious belief and class deference. There were three overlapping causes for this. In the first place, the sheer number of extra children born in the post-war era meant there were many more adolescents in the 1960s and 1970s – and the cohesion of this group was accentuated in a number of countries (such as Britain) by the introduction of compulsory secondary education up to at least the age of fifteen (Marwick 2011: 31). Second, the rise in economic prosperity in these years meant that teenagers had much more disposable income, which helped to inspire a distinct 'youth culture', organized particularly around new film and music, often from or inspired by the United States. Films like *Rebel without a Cause* (1955) and *The Wild One* (1953), which dramatized youth violence and generational tension, were good examples, while the music of Elvis Presley and later the Beatles inspired hordes of teenage fans (Gassert 2014: 190–1). Third, the rise in the number of young people attending university also encouraged a greater questioning of social norms as well as increasing the potential for political radicalism – despite, or perhaps because of, a political environment that could be suffocatingly conservative due to the atmosphere of the Cold War, particularly in the United States. The net result was a situation in which, although the spread of progressive values was far from universal and unilinear (so that, for example, adherence to religious values remained far higher in the United States than in Western Europe in the 1960s and 1970s), important changes occurred at both a cultural and legislative level. In particular the new generation tended to desire greater individual freedom, especially in terms of gender and sexuality – so that there were demands for the legalization of abortion, for greater acceptance (or legalization) of homosexuality, and for greater equality for women. But there was also a strong demand for racial equality, with the Civil Rights Act (1964) and Voting Rights Act (1965) being passed in the United States, and the Race Relations Acts of 1965, 1968 and 1976 in Britain, while other political radicals focused their energies on opposing the proliferation of nuclear weapons or the escalation of the Vietnam War (Marwick 2011: 241, 359, 510–30, 683–6).

In this situation, conservatives were presented with new opportunities but also with significant new challenges. On the positive side, the fact that post-war social democracy and universal welfare states encountered serious practical difficulties in the 1970s offered conservatives new possibilities – not least because this exposed some of the ambiguities used to justify them. (When government money became scarcer, difficult questions about what constituted a genuinely just distribution of resources arose much more urgently than before.) But more negatively, conservatives were also alarmed by the libertarianism of the 1960s, which often seemed to represent a wholesale rejection of tradition, by questioning the nuclear family, conventional religion and the importance of patriotism, and thereby making a controlled approach to change impossible. And if some fears about the future now seem misplaced, even risible – such as conservative worries in 1970s Britain that the electorate was liable to become 'proletarianized' (Hutber 1977) – others, particularly the fear that greater 'permissiveness' would ultimately cause religious decline, seem much more prescient (Brown 2001).

Alongside the continuation of some previous conservative strategies, there were arguably five main conservative responses in this period. By far the most important was that associated with the 'New Right', which we will examine first in detail. The other four types, by contrast, all to some extent represented reactions to this form of conservatism. Thus, the second was a traditionalist response in the 1970s and 1980s, particularly in Britain, that was much warier of the market; the third a qualified critique of New Right conservatism in the 1990s and 2000s, from sympathetic yet critical observers of how it had operated in practice; the fourth a neo-conservative response to New Right foreign policy; and the fifth a more recent form of 'populist' conservatism, which arguably has a much more questionable claim to being labelled as 'conservative' at all. We will examine each in turn. Before proceeding, we should note again that the focus of this chapter is almost exclusively Anglo-American, partly for reasons of space, but mainly because the most interesting developments in conservatism in this era have tended to be in Britain or the USA.[2]

Conservative Response I: New Right Conservatism

First, then, let us consider the type of conservatism that emerged from the 'New Right' movement. Doing so raises both substantive and definitional questions, because the New Right was a complex and multi-stranded phenomenon, taking inspiration from a wide range of intellectual sources. Amongst others, these included the Virginia school of political economy, which argued against the idea that political actors were motivated by the same impulses as those in the economic sphere; libertarians inspired by the political philosopher Robert Nozick's claim that political legitimacy derived from pre-political property rights; and monetarists influenced by the economist Milton Friedman's argument that inflation was primarily caused by the amount of money in the economy. Conversely, the New Right also included thinkers like the British politician Lord Coleraine, who criticized universal welfare states for removing the incentive for individuals to support themselves; and, particularly in the United States, representatives of the so-called 'moral majority', including the evangelist Jerry Falwell, who felt that the permissive society had undermined proper moral values (Peele 1984; Gray 1993; Neill 2019). Traditionally, this has meant that analysts have tended to distinguish between neo-liberal and neo-conservative aspects of the New Right, differentiating between those who seek to uphold individual liberty for its own sake, and those who do so because it impels individuals to be more moral, to take personal responsibility for themselves. While such a distinction is not valueless, since there certainly have been New Right theorists who were more purely libertarian than others, arguably it does not capture the distinction between 'liberal' and 'conservative' here entirely accurately. For even some of those New Right theorists labelled 'liberal' or 'libertarian' often had highly conservative facets to their thought, on the definition we have been working with – namely that they sought to control change and appealed to the operation of an 'extra-human' order.

A case in point is the well-known and influential Austrian

émigré economist and social theorist F. A. Hayek. Famous for arguing for economic and political liberty in *The Road to Serfdom* (1944), and, in less lurid terms, in a series of texts including *The Constitution of Liberty* (1960) and *Law, Legislation, and Liberty* (1973–9), Hayek is often labelled a 'libertarian' rather than a conservative. This is because (it is claimed) Hayek's arguments were primarily based upon the epistemic superiority of the market in securing optimal economic outcomes for individuals (as opposed to the state's attempts to plan for them). Furthermore, insofar as he connected such arguments with morality, he did so in order to uphold a conception of human dignity posited in fairly universal, ahistorical terms. But such arguments only tell half the story. Despite the fact that even Hayek himself self-consciously disclaimed the adjective 'conservative', there were at least two definitely conservative aspects to his thought. In the first place, Hayek stressed the importance of *evolutionary change* – of history and tradition as the repository of collective human wisdom, and hence as the source of guidelines for the successful adaptation of human relationships. Such evolutionary change, Hayek argued, had gradually provided us with a harmonious 'spontaneous order' as a framework for human action. This functioned in classic conservative fashion as an 'extra-human' context for individual actions and choices (Gray 1984: 42; Freeden 1996: 302). Second, on a related point, Hayek's conception of reason was more conservative than liberal: rather than offering the possibility of self-consciously formulating individual or communal ends, or of shaping the human evolutionary process, reason was relegated to the job of evaluating existing practices. To quote Hayek himself: 'human reason can neither predict nor deliberately shape its own future. Its advances consist in finding out where it has been wrong' (Hayek 1960: 41).[3] In other words, if Hayek, as he claimed, was restating the principles of classical liberals, he unquestionably did so in a distinctly conservative manner.

New Right conservatism in Britain: Thatcherism

What, then, characterized New Right conservatism? To determine this, while examining thinkers like Hayek is revealing, arguably the most promising method is to consider how it developed in practice in Britain and the United States, where it was prosecuted in an unusually ideologically self-conscious manner. (This was one of the reasons behind the coining of the term 'Thatcherism' in Britain, and to a lesser extent 'Reaganism' in the United States.) Of course, given the diversity of intellectual influences behind the conservatism of the New Right, and the different people involved in enacting it, a certain amount of variation within the ideology was inevitable; nevertheless examining it reveals a reasonably consistent position. So, taking Thatcherism in Britain as an example, we find this was organized around four key arguments.

First, most importantly, Thatcherites took it as a fundamental tenet that post-war conservatives had misdiagnosed the nature of the challenge posed by social democracy between 1945 and the 1970s, acceding far too readily to the argument that it was necessary for the state to co-operate with trade unions, to intervene in the economy to prevent unemployment, and to own key industries, in order to preserve social harmony and manage change successfully. At best, Thatcherites contended, such positions were (partially) excusable accommodations to an unpromising economic and political environment, but much more common was the claim that conservative thinkers and politicians in the post-war era had betrayed the party's tradition, so that it was necessary to denounce the mistakes of the recent past, and seek inspiration from earlier, more authentic conservatism (Green 1999: 20–1). At their extreme, such denunciations became practically a conversion experience, so that Sir Keith Joseph, one of Margaret Thatcher's mentors, famously declared in 1975 that he had only become a genuine conservative in April 1974 – since, as he put it, 'I had thought I was a Conservative but now I see that I was not really one at all' (Wright 2013: 43). It is true that there was some debate amongst Thatcherites as to where the trouble had first started. Thus Margaret Thatcher herself – despite often lauding 'Victorian values' – was arguably most interested in rehabilitating the Britain of the 1930s, while Lord Coleraine was not alone in blaming Stanley Baldwin for the gradual slide into corporatism and statism (Green 1999: 19–21; Neill 2019: 172–3). But all were united in their disapproval of post-war conservatism, and in claiming that they were returning conservatism to its authentic path.

If the first aspect of Thatcherism was its insistence that the conservative tradition itself had erred in its diagnosis of the post-war progressive challenge, the second was an insistence on the importance of individual personal responsibility, and of the correct limits to state power. To some extent such arguments resembled those of late nineteenth-century theorists like Herbert Spencer, in that they attempted to use previously liberal ideas for conservative purposes, but these were necessarily posed in a quite different idiom, given the growth of the size of the state and changes in British society. Essentially, what the Thatcherites sought to do was to re-establish what they saw as the proper scope for individual liberty, which they felt had been menaced from a number of directions by the post-war state. The threats had included the compulsory membership of trade unions, state intervention in incomes policy, and high rates of inflation and direct income tax (which adversely affected an individual's ability to spend their own money). In addition, they argued that the attempt by government to intervene so extensively in so many areas had, paradoxically, reduced its authority. As the 1979 Conservative election manifesto put it: by 'attempting to do too much, politicians have failed to do those things which should be done. This has damaged the country and the authority of the government' (Conservative Manifesto 1979: 7). To remedy this, the Thatcher governments launched a two-pronged approach. Firstly, they put forward a series of measures designed to increase individual liberty. These included measures to reduce direct taxes, decrease the level of inflation, and gradually reduce the power of trade unions (through the abolition of the 'closed shop' and the imposition of strike ballots). More positively, they sought to encourage home ownership (through mortgage incentives and the selling of council houses) and the ownership of shares in private companies (Evans 1997: 24–39). Secondly, however, they also sought to reinforce the authority of the state, by increasing spending on defence and the police, limiting centrally the amount local government could spend, and, in the 1990s, making the criminal justice system more punitive (Evans 1997: 95, 75; Farrall and Jennings 2014: 213–14).

Part of the point of increasing individual liberty, as far as Thatcherites were concerned, was simply to improve economic performance – because, they reasoned, if individuals had more control of their money, they would have more incentive to be productive. But their third key argument was that granting individuals more liberty would also make them more *moral*, by encouraging them to take greater responsibility for themselves. If individuals had to rely on their own resources to ensure their own security and self-development, the Thatcherites argued, they were much more likely to develop what the conservative political theorist Shirley Robin Letwin called the 'vigorous virtues' of self-reliance, moral responsibility and independent-mindedness (Letwin 1992: 13–16). By contrast, if their needs were wholly or largely provided for by the state, as in the post-war era, then individuals were far less likely to take care of themselves or others – particularly given the influence of the 'permissive society', with its disdain for traditional moral values. Subsequent commentators, including some contemporary analysts, have pointed out that there was a potential contradiction in this advocacy of 'individualism', since Thatcherites seemed to be extolling both the vision of the cautious, thrifty individual on the one hand, and the flamboyant, buccaneering risk-taker on the other (Grimley 2012: 93). But in the 1970s and 1980s, such tensions were largely subsumed within the Thatcherite determination to dismantle the norms of post-war social democracy and all that this entailed.

Finally, however, it is important to emphasize that Thatcherism did not simply advocate individualism without qualification. As with all types of conservative ideology, it maintained that ultimately individual volition should be subject to the core concept of an 'extra-human' order, which constrains the way in which individual freedom should be exercised. In the economic sphere, the extra-human sanction was provided by the market itself – or more precisely by the epistemic difficulty that Thatcherites claimed existed in trying to gain genuine knowledge of the myriad number of economic choices under modern capitalism. (This was an argument the Thatcherites borrowed from Hayek, though they were much more wary of the corollary Hayek himself thought followed from it – namely that the income gained by successful market players had little to do with desert.) More widely, Thatcherites argued that individual decision-making should be constrained by the 'natural' institutions provided by tradition, namely the family and the nation – both of which they claimed had been threatened by the 'permissive' values of the 1960s, with its stress on sexual freedom and criticism of the Vietnam War. Thus the 1987 Conservative election manifesto declared that 'the desire to do better for one's family is one of the strongest motives in human nature', while Margaret Thatcher's own stress on 'Britain' and 'the nation', always strong, only increased in fervour after the victory in the Falklands War against Argentina in 1982 (Conservative Manifesto 1987: 27; Gamble 1994: 26–7; Letwin 1992: 36–7). In doing so, Thatcherism recycled themes used earlier in the twentieth century, not least by Baldwin, as we saw in Chapter 4. And like Baldwin too, the Thatcherites tended to weaponize such contrasts against their opponents, claiming that the Labour Party in the 1980s was suspect on the issue of patriotism (given its equivocations over the desirability of nuclear weapons) and on the institution of the nuclear family (given its greater sympathy for such groups as single mothers and for gay and lesbian liberation). If the tactic was updated for a new set of historical circumstances, in other words, it was nevertheless an ideologically familiar one.

New Right conservatism in the USA

These developments in Britain had clear counterparts in the United States, where the inauguration of Ronald Reagan as president in 1981 marked the culmination of a long struggle by conservatives to be taken seriously after the post-war hegemony of 'big government' liberalism, exemplified above all by Lyndon Johnson's 'Great Society' programmes in the 1960s. As in Britain, these programmes had been underpinned by a 'golden age' of economic growth and the supposed success of Keynesian demand management. Thus, as in Britain, New Right conservatism, long out of intellectual and political fashion, seized the opportunity presented by the economic travails of the 1970s to gain power in the 1980s and enact robustly conservative policies. In particular, the Reagan administration succeeded in passing a set of tax cuts through Congress in 1981 and 1986, reducing the highest personal tax rate from 70 per cent to 50 per cent and then 28 per cent, and the lowest from 14 per cent to 11 per cent. It also substantially weakened the power of organized labour, after Reagan's confrontation with the air traffic controllers' union, PATCO, in which he threatened to fire nearly 13,000 controllers, thereby emboldening private sector employers to follow the same tactics (Hoover and Plant 2015: 33–6; McCartin 2013).

In parallel with the aims of the New Right in Britain, the purpose of such economic liberalization was not simply to increase productivity, but also to reinforce traditional moral values – particularly those of the nuclear family. For such values, conservatives in the United States claimed, had been menaced not only by onset of the permissive society, and most notoriously by the legalization of abortion in 1973, but also by the pernicious phenomenon of 'welfare dependency'. Far from making American society more civilized, such conservatives argued, in language Shirley Robin Letwin would have heartily approved of, these developments in fact encouraged moral delinquency by shielding individuals from the consequences of their actions. Thus, as the conservative political scientist Lawrence M. Mead wrote in his 1986 book *Beyond Entitlement: The Social Obligations of Citizenship*, the recipients of federal welfare 'seldom have to work or otherwise function to earn whatever income, service, or benefit a program gives; meager though it may be, they receive it essentially as an entitlement'. '[T]his lack of accountability', Mead continued, was a key reason why 'nonwork, crime, family breakup, and other problems are much commoner among recipients than Americans generally' (Mead 1986: 9, 70). Or, as the controversial political scientist Charles Murray put it even more sharply: 'when the government intervenes to help … it not only diminishes our responsibility for the desired outcome, it enfeebles the institutions through which people live satisfying lives' (Murray 2012: 285).

There was therefore a strong degree of overlap between the progress of the New Right in Britain and that in the United States. But there were also four significant differences, which, although they certainly do not negate the grouping of British and American forms of the New Right together, should nevertheless be noted. First, the degree to which anti-communism and the Cold War underpinned the New Right in the United States was arguably greater than in Britain. For if there was no doubt that such conservatives in Britain were firmly anti-communist, and even that they occasionally tried to equate the degree of the Labour government's control with that of Warsaw Pact countries in the 1970s, the extent to which anti-communism animated New Right conservatism in the United States was nevertheless still greater. Partly due to the pre-eminent role the United States shouldered as leader of the free world in the Cold War, but more viscerally because of the trauma of the Vietnam War and before that of 'losing China' to communism in 1949, opposition to communism became an absolute bedrock of New Right conservatism in the United States. So important was this to such conservatives that they criticized not only the attempts to reduce international tension and develop a modus vivendi with the USSR in the 1970s through détente, but even President Nixon's policy of trying to encircle the Soviet Union by making common cause with China. Though widely lauded as a diplomatic masterstroke at the time, for conservatives like the influential commentator and author William F. Buckley, such a policy represented a terrible betrayal, since it involved making common cause with an immoral communist power (Hoeveler 1991: 45). Hence, too, the impetus for President Reagan's massive increase in military spending in the 1980s, despite this significantly contributing to budget deficits, an outcome New Right conservatives would otherwise have surely damned as utterly irresponsible.

Second, although disapproval of the 'permissive society' formed an important part of New Right conservatism in Britain, such opposition was even more emphatic in the United States. There were two main reasons for this. In the first place, many of the legal changes that transformed social legislation in the USA in the 1960s and 1970s were in fact enacted by the Supreme Court, rather than legislatively, as in Britain. Such changes included barring prayer from public schools (1962); making the prosecution of obscenity much harder (1964), legalizing the birth control pill (1965);

granting the right to remain silent and to consult an attorney when arrested (1966); and, most momentously, the legalization of abortion in *Roe v. Wade* (1973) (Micklethwait and Wooldridge 2004: 308–13). This made it much easier for New Right conservatives to claim that such changes were made in defiance of American public opinion, rather than in harmony with it. It also, more intellectually, induced conservatives to seek the appointment of judges who were committed to an 'originalist' interpretation of the constitution – in other words, who claimed that the constitution could be interpreted fairly literally, without recourse to interpretation to update it to present circumstances, let alone with reference to other (foreign) legal systems.[4] In the second place, the higher degree of religious belief in the United States meant that opposition to 'permissiveness' was much easier to organize. One level of such opposition was intellectual. Thus, partly inspired by the writings of Leo Strauss, and partly by a conservative interpretation of Catholic doctrine, some conservatives cited natural law as a reason to oppose some of the 'lifestyles' being promoted by permissive liberals (Strauss 1953; MacIntyre 1985). It was contended, for example, that because both nature and the Bible decreed that life began at conception, and that only sexual intercourse between men and women was legitimate, both abortion and homosexuality were profoundly wrong. More practically, in the 1970s the increasing willingness of American evangelical Christians to commit to explicitly political conservatism provided the basis for a powerful movement to oppose permissive liberal values. Dubbed the 'moral majority' by one of its organizers, Paul Weyrich, this movement spawned a host of influential organizations and prominent individuals, but two in particular perhaps deserve special mention.

One was Phyllis Schlafly, who came to prominence through her outspoken support for the conservative Barry Goldwater's doomed run for the presidency against Lyndon Johnson in 1964, summarized in her text *A Choice, Not an Echo*, and through her radio show *Wake Up, America*. As a result of Schlafly's considerable organizing efforts, the attempt by feminists to pass an Equal Rights Amendment to the constitution was defeated, and despite other feminist victories, the ERA still remains unpassed to the present day.

The second was Jerry Falwell, who campaigned against racial desegregation in the 1960s, and who founded Liberty University in 1971. Clearly already active in the conservative movement, Falwell came to particular prominence in 1978, after the Internal Revenue Service proposed depriving all private schools set up after 1953 of their tax-deductible status on the grounds they were discriminatory – when the majority of such schools in the south of the United States were Christian ones. Largely through Falwell's efforts, President Carter's administration and congressional representatives were bombarded with campaigning letters, with the result that the IRS eventually dropped the proposal. For Falwell, this was but one example of the moral predicament the USA was in, so that religious involvement in politics was vital – for if 'Satan had mobilized his forces to destroy America', it logically followed that 'God needed voices raised to save the nation from inner moral decay' (Micklethwait and Wooldridge 2004: 80–5).

The third reason that New Right conservatism was different in the United States compared to Britain relates to issues of race. As we saw in Chapter 2, southern conservatism in the USA in the early to mid-nineteenth century was intimately bound up with issues of race and slavery, the rights of states against the federal government, and the question of how to define genuine 'freedom' in the context of a rapidly industrializing society. Obviously, the nature of American society had changed enormously by the 1960s. Nevertheless, despite the abolition of slavery after the defeat of the southern Confederacy in the 1861–5 Civil War, the failure of 'Reconstruction' after that war to guarantee genuinely equal rights to African Americans in practice – due to states being permitted to pass discriminatory laws, known as 'Jim Crow' – meant that race remained very much a live issue in the USA in the 1960s. This was the context within which Lyndon Johnson secured the enactment of the landmark Civil Rights Act (1964) and Voting Rights Act (1965), which finally granted something approaching genuine equality to African Americans, and created both opportunities and challenges for New Right conservatives. On a practical political level, it created an opportunity for Republicans to win electoral victories in southern states, an opportunity first seized by

Richard Nixon in the presidential election of 1968, but increasingly replicated by Republicans at both presidential and congressional elections ever since (Black and Black 2002). (There were of course some important exceptions, such as Jimmy Carter's success in southern states in the presidential election of 1976, but this does not negate the trend.) On a more theoretical level, what conservatives were seeking to uphold was more complex, sometimes even contradictory, and divided essentially into three different reactions.

In the first place, in opposing the Civil Rights Act, some conservatives were seeking to defend the rights of states against the federal government, to some extent reproducing arguments culled from nineteenth-century conservatism. Rather than mounting explicitly racial arguments, in other words, they claimed to be simply defending a traditional set of constitutional arrangements against federal government encroachment (Peele 1984: 132–3). This is not of course to suggest that there were not conservatives who both advocated states' rights against the federal government *and* were clearly racist – Jesse Helms, senator for North Carolina from 1973 to 2003, who opposed all civil rights legislation and supported the apartheid regime in South Africa, was but the most prominent example. Secondly, other conservatives objected to the civil rights legislation of the 1960s on grounds that resembled the arguments of Michael Oakeshott – namely that such legislation was justified and enacted on a rationalist basis, rather than respecting and building upon concrete historical reality. Thus Buckley, in his 1959 text *Up from Liberalism*, argued that liberals had made civil rights exclusively a matter of abstract rational ideals, rather than seeking to respect and encourage the thriving ethnic culture that had actually allowed the black community to advance (Buckley 1959: 155–67). And finally, much more controversially, some conservatives such as Charles Murray and Richard Hernstein in *The Bell Curve: Intelligence and Class Structure in American Life* (1994) came close to positing genetic differences between whites and non-whites, claiming that 'it seems highly likely to us that both genes and the environment have something to do with racial differences' (Hernstein and Murray 1994: 311). Such statements, unsurprisingly, have been fiercely attacked by both scientists and social commentators alike – but leaving that on one side there is no doubt that Hernstein and Murray sought to justify their arguments in a quintessentially conservative fashion, positing a pseudo-scientific justification for racial difference in order to resist and manage momentous social and historical change. To say that race was more of a key issue for New Right conservatives in the United States is not of course to claim that it was irrelevant in Britain. The prominent Conservative MP Enoch Powell, whose thought has often been seen as a forerunner to Thatcherism, made a notorious speech warning about the perils of non-white immigration in 1968,[5] which evoked a strong positive response from a section of the white working class; while Margaret Thatcher herself publicly worried about the possibility of Britain being 'swamped by people of a different culture' when talking about immigration from the Commonwealth and Pakistan in 1978 (Schofield 2012: 106). But such episodes were generally the exception rather than the rule, and this was also true of the final issue which generally occupied the New Right in the USA much more than in Britain in the 1970s and 1980s – namely anti-Establishment populism. It is true that this had its place within Thatcherism. Part of Margaret Thatcher's appeal to sections of the lower middle class and unionized working class who traditionally had not voted Tory was to position herself as an 'outsider' who was not part of the traditional London 'Establishment', even within the Conservative Party; and her unembarrassed sloganizing about British greatness certainly marked a sharp divide from the traditional post-war language of political debate. Nevertheless, anti-elitist populism was a much more significant component of New Right conservatism in the United States.

There were essentially three variants of this, but all converged in the post-war context in hostility towards a north-eastern 'establishment', which conservatives felt (with some justification) dominated the major universities, media, diplomatic service and both major political parties – Republican as well as Democrat. The first variant stemmed from a phenomenon we have mentioned already – namely southern resentment, which was particularly ignited by the passing of civil rights legislation in the 1960s, but more generally stemmed from a feeling that northern politicians were contemptuous of the traditions of the south, whether they be the symbols of the old Confederacy, or the fervent evangelical religiosity of the so-called 'Bible Belt'. The second variant, epitomized by the doomed (but prophetic) presidential candidacy of the Arizonan Barry Goldwater in 1964, was western resentment at the north-eastern 'establishment'. Drawing on the traditional idea of rugged individualists building a life for themselves on the western frontier in the nineteenth century, such westerners stressed the importance of libertarianism as well as evangelical Christianity, favouring cars over public transport, bungalows over apartment blocks, and in general contrasting their genuinely free lives with those of Americans back east, dominated by a banking elite, union bosses and, above all, the federal government (McGirr 2001).[6] Finally, the fully fledged version of such rhetoric, which had bloomed by the 1980s, saw anti-Establishment populism deployed against a huge array of anti-conservative targets, as for example in the influential book *The Establishment vs. the People* (1983), written by the indefatigable author and organizer Richard Viguerie. Scathing about the performance of traditional elites, on account of their corruption, failure to offer moral leadership and remoteness from the values of ordinary Americans, Viguerie's book offered a full-scale denunciation of big government, big business, the educational and legal establishments and traditional media outlets. It castigated big business for doing corrupt deals with government to prevent genuine market competition, attacked the National Education Association for failing to respect parents' desire for the 'basics', and denounced the legal profession for its obscurantism and failure to provide ordinary citizens with genuine justice (amongst many other charges) (Hoeveler 1991: 8–9). Thus, by the 1980s, such populist resentment formed a significant component of American New Right conservatism.

Conservative Response II: Traditionalism

If New Right conservatism was the most influential new form of the ideology to appear in response to the changed circumstances of the last three decades of the twentieth century, it was far from being the only important one, even in an Anglo-American context. As we have seen, what united all forms of New Right conservatism in Britain and the United States was a belief that liberalizing the market would have beneficial consequences – that at the very least it would improve economic productivity, and might well also encourage individuals to become more moral, by giving them an incentive to take responsibility for themselves. But for a second group of conservatives, found particularly in Britain, such a strong stress on market freedom – or indeed liberty more generally – was a mistake, since it misdiagnosed the primary problem that confronted conservatives in the 1970s and 1980s. This was because for such conservatives, often labelled 'traditionalists' or 'authoritarians', the major problem was not primarily the illegitimate increase in the power of the state, or overmighty trade unions illicitly interfering in market transactions, but rather the assault on traditional moral values enabled by the rise of permissiveness, and the decrease in respect for traditional authority in general. As such, although often originally part of the 'New Right' themselves (broadly conceived), such thinkers looked with suspicion on Thatcherite and Reaganite solutions that prioritized individual liberty, arguing that such solutions were too *liberal*, and were over-obsessed with the threat of socialism or communism, when in fact the most important threat came from liberalism itself.[7] In pointed contrast to politicians like Margaret Thatcher, in other words – whom traditionalists felt were too impressed by the experiences of Soviet émigrés like Alexander Solzhenitsyn, and by the laissez-faire liberalism of the nineteenth century – such conservatives stressed the importance of reaffirming the values of tradition and authority. As one of them, the British journalist Peregrine Worsthorne, wrote in 1978: 'the spectre haunting most ordinary people in Britain is neither of a totalitarian state nor of Big Brother, but of ordinary people being allowed to run wild. What they are worried about is crime, violence, disorder in schools, promiscuity, idleness, pornography, football hooliganism, vandalism and urban terrorism'. As the title of his essay provocatively put it, the real problem was 'too much freedom' (Worsthorne 1978: 150).

What, then, did the traditionalist conservatives suggest to ameliorate this situation? Taking Britain first, it must be noted that their arguments in this context, particularly in the 1970s, tended to smack of some pessimism. This was because the main group advocating traditionalism – namely Worsthorne, the historian Maurice Cowling, the literary critic John Casey, the religious historian Edward Norman and the philosopher Roger Scruton, all of whom had connections to Cambridge University – thought the problems identified by the Thatcherite and Reaganite New Right ran deeper than that movement had realized. In the first place, they believed that the individualism and moral pluralism unleashed by the 'permissive' values of the 1960s had done such serious damage to common moral standards, and to the instinctive respect for hierarchical social structures, that it would be very difficult for the state to regain its proper authority. Because such fundamental disagreement over moral values had developed, in other words, trying to uphold the authority of law on the basis of citizens' having reasonably similar moral intuitions was very difficult to maintain – even on the limited basis that Oakeshott had recommended (Neill 2019: 171). Secondly, they worried that the permissive society had induced modern citizens to prioritize the 'tender' virtues of compassion at the expense of the 'vigorous' virtues of self-reliance, and unlike the Thatcherites they were sceptical that solely economic remedies could reverse this process. As such, the traditionalists reasserted the importance of tradition and hierarchy in a manner somewhat reminiscent of T. S. Eliot, though they were rarely as critical of the effects of capitalism as Eliot had been; they simply thought that expecting economic liberalization to fix social problems was profoundly to miss the point.

We can see this if we examine Roger Scruton's *The Meaning of Conservatism* (1980), probably the most developed statement of traditionalism in this period, where he argued for three fundamental positions in particular. First, Scruton claimed that the authority of the state does not come from the consent of individuals, or because it agrees to guarantee their liberty, but rather because individuals can only truly realize themselves as an organic part of it.[8] As Scruton himself put it: 'the condition of man requires that the individual, while he exists and acts as an autonomous being, does so only because he can first identify himself as something greater' (Scruton 2001: 24). Second, Scruton argued that this meant the state was entirely justified in legislating about the private morals of individuals – since the idea that individuals had rights prior to the formation of the state was based upon a false premise. As such, asking why the state should have the right to interfere in an individual's private conduct, as the advocates of the 'permissive society' had done, was to pose completely the wrong question. Instead, Scruton maintained, individuals know intuitively that certain forms of behaviour (such as pornography and television violence) are simply wrong in and of themselves (Scruton 2001: 68–70). Finally, Scruton argued strongly against the idea that aesthetic judgement was purely a matter of individual taste, railing against 'the rot of pluralism'. On the contrary, what the best of our tradition had bequeathed us was an invaluable store of (high) cultural knowledge, and it was vital that this was defended against cultural relativism. According to Scruton, in other words, support for the best of traditional high culture was crucial to defending a properly functioning traditional, hierarchical society (Scruton 1978: 113).

Traditionalist conservatism in Britain thus had a certain influence in the 1970s and 1980s, not least because Scruton's activities also included founding a journal, the *Salisbury Review*, to popularize the traditionalists' values. Nevertheless, their influence tended to be diluted in the 1980s, partly because their suspicion of Margaret Thatcher's patriotism was significantly allayed by her decision to go to war to defend the Falkland Islands in 1982, but also because the Thatcherites were, in any case, politically successful enough to ignore the traditionalists when the latter's message became uncongenial to them.

In the United States, traditionalist conservatism was in general even less appealing – almost certainly because the project of resuscitating traditional moral values was more firmly integrated into the message of New Right conservatism itself. There was, nevertheless, one influential American traditionalist who should be noted, partly because he played such an important role in founding two influential conservative journals in the post-war period, namely the *National*

Review and *Modern Age*, but also because he was one of the first to challenge the orthodoxy in that era that no genuine conservative tradition existed in the United States – as opposed to a liberal one.[9] This was the writer and organizer Russell Kirk, who wrote a wide array of texts about conservatism, as well as a fair amount of fiction, but was most famous for his book *The Conservative Mind* (1953). Kirk argued that, rather than there being no American conservative tradition, the country had in fact had notable conservatives since the very founding of the republic, including John Adams and Alexander Hamilton, as well as notable ones since, including Alexis de Tocqueville, Nathaniel Hawthorne, Irving Babbitt and George Santayana. Quite as much as Britain and France, therefore, the USA had had a very strong conservative tradition, stressing above all the importance of divine order, hierarchy and tradition in contrast to radical beliefs in the power of abstract reasoning, the perfectibility of man, and economic and political levelling. If few subsequent American conservatives followed the detail of Kirk's arguments – unsurprisingly given his suspicion of capitalism, and of that icon of the American free market, the motor car – his dogged insistence that US conservatives had their own tradition to sustain them against liberals and radicals nevertheless still proved influential (Kirk 2008).

Conservative Response III: Post-New Right Conservatism – David Willetts, John Gray, Jesse Norman

There is no question that New Right conservatism proved highly successful, both politically and intellectually, in the 1980s and 1990s. Politically, the Conservative Party in Britain won four general elections in a row, from 1979 to 1992; in the United States, the Republicans won three presidential elections (in 1980, 1984 and 1988), and control of the House of Representatives in 1994 for the first time in forty years. On an intellectual level, even more significantly, New Right conservatism was clearly hegemonic in this period. Thus in Britain, ideological opponents of Thatcherism struggled to formulate convincing alternatives, since both traditional social democracy and the more interventionist and strongly redistributive approaches on the Left appeared obsolete in an era of greater globalization and a rapidly changing labour market. This meant that the only way the Labour Party was able to win power in 1997 was by jettisoning overt egalitarianism and extra spending (Heffernan 2000). In the United States, New Right conservatism appeared if anything even more dominant. The dramatic Republican capture of the House of Representatives in 1994 was achieved by campaigning on the basis of an explicitly New Right conservative document, the 'Contract with America', and had such force that it impelled the Democratic president Bill Clinton to declare that 'the era of big government is over' in his State of the Union address in 1996.

However, the era also presented new problems for conservatives. To focus on Britain, a common complaint by conservative thinkers in the 1990s and 2000s was that although Thatcherism had been supposed to reduce state control over civil society, in practice it had if anything increased it – in areas like education, health and social security – through regulations, targets and the imposition of spending limits. These critics tended to accept, albeit often grudgingly, that there had been some justification for more government centralization in the early 1980s, since it was the only way to bring illicit organizations like trade unions and unrepresentative local government under control. But they still objected strongly to the tendency of the later Thatcher governments to try to manage aspects of society that had previously been the province of voluntary groups, local government or the private sector, on the basis that this would damage long-standing beneficial traditions within civil society.

Some of those complaining about centralization reasoned that the problems were largely the product of difficult economic circumstances and bad political decision-making, rather than having much to do with the fundamental worth of New Right conservatism. The conservative author and MP David Willetts, for example, lamented the way in which Conservative governments had enacted legislation such as the Children Act (1989) and the Food Safety Act (1990), on the basis that these were restrictive and heavy-handed; nonetheless, he thought that Thatcherism was only at fault to the extent that it had failed to reverse the existing trend towards centralization that had been present since the Second World War (Willetts 1997: 128, 78). (Willetts damned, in particular, the centralized nature of the post-war welfare state, and the way in which post-war housing estates had been constructed.) Certainly, he did not blame Thatcherite economic policies, arguing instead for the compatibility – and indeed the supportive and symbiotic relationship – of a globalized free market and a flourishing civil society. But a number of other conservatives, including the political philosopher John Gray and the author and MP Jesse Norman, disagreed, claiming to a greater or lesser extent that the economic policies pursued by the New Right had caused conservatism more fundamental problems. We will briefly look at Gray and Norman in turn.

Taking Gray first, we discover a thinker who had become profoundly dissatisfied with the nature of the New Right by the late 1990s. Previously an enthusiast for economic liberalization, and the author of sympathetic books on Mill and Hayek in the 1980s, by the turn of the millennium when he wrote 'The Undoing of Conservatism' (1997) Gray had become profoundly dissatisfied with how the Thatcher and Reagan administrations had governed in practice. This was because, whatever the intentions of the more conservative elements of the New Right, what had in fact happened was that governments had assumed that all political problems could be solved by the continual expansion of unfettered, competitive markets. This was a position Gray labelled 'free-market fundamentalism', and he argued that it had three implications that were all intensely damaging to genuine conservatism. First, articulating a worry that went all the way back to Burke, Gray charged that unfettered markets tended to undermine the very conditions that made them possible, by erasing the distinctiveness of local institutions and thereby eliminating the local knowledge that was inherent to them. In this way, unfettered capitalism encouraged a dreary cultural uniformity, rather than genuine civilization for all, creating a historical breach with the past which ultimately destroyed the very sensitivity to individual differences that was one of the major strengths of the market in the first place (Gray 1997b: 40–1).

Second, Gray claimed that 'free-market fundamentalism' encouraged a utopian mindset which assumed that permanent universal progress was possible – whereas in fact true conservatives should accept that humans are necessarily imperfect creatures, and that any progress would be limited and infinitely variable, according to the culture involved (Gray 1997b: 41–3). Finally, and most fundamentally, Gray argued that free-market fundamentalism also encouraged an entirely false picture of individuals as being capable of making meaningful choices with little reference to their cultural backgrounds. Indeed, Gray went even further, floating the idea that even subtler versions of arguments for liberal autonomy – those that *did* admit that autonomous choices could only be made with reference to a given cultural background – might be a mistake. On that basis, only a much more culturally relativist position, which accepted that there could be unbridgeable cultural differences over fundamental political concepts like liberty and community, could be genuinely conservative (Gray 1997b: 43–5, 45–6). While Gray did not commit himself unequivocally to such a position, his overall argument was clear: by ignoring the importance of tradition and cultural difference, the New Right had acted in a way that was highly damaging to modern society's cultural resources, and had presented a vision of the individual self that was fundamentally incoherent.

Gray's conclusion at this time was fairly depressive: such was the damage that 'free-market fundamentalism' had done, it was very difficult to envisage a solution for conservatives. By contrast, Jesse Norman, a Conservative MP since 2010, but also the author of books on Burke and Adam Smith, and editor of a set of essays on Oakeshott, was more hopeful about conservative prospects for the future. He too, however, in his book *The Big Society* (2010), was critical of some of the same aspects of Thatcherism as Gray. Writing at the end of a long period of Labour government between 1997 and 2010, Norman was deeply critical of its record, claiming that it had combined the illusion of strong economic performance (based upon high public borrowing, unsustainable private debt, and cheap imported labour) with a deeply unattractive centralized welfare system (which was both high-handed and inefficient, confusing as well as micro-managing its recipients) (Norman 2010: 19–25; Neill 2020). But he argued that some of these problems also had their roots in the Thatcherite period in government, contending, like Gray, that the fault lay not merely in the latter's tendency to centralization, but more deeply in its social and economic philosophy. Thus he argued, as Gray had done, that because Thatcherism had tended to conceptualize human beings as rational, ahistorical, self-interested individuals, intent only on maximizing their own pleasure, this had inevitably led to a neglect of civil society institutions (Norman 2010: 45, 51–8). In other words, because individuals were deemed to make choices on an instrumentalist basis, there was little reason to respect the role of civil society institutions in explaining how individuals formulated their preferences in the first place or in helping to achieve them – since the central state, being much more powerful, had an infinitely greater ability to secure immediate individual wants (Norman 2010: 70).

However, at this point Norman departed from Gray, contending that there were still definite solutions to these problems for conservatives. Theoretically, he argued, instead of conceptualizing individuals as merely pleasure maximizers, it was vital to understand them as active entities with various 'capabilities', so that the aim of public policy should be to try to fulfil these as far as possible. Such capabilities, according to Norman, borrowing from the economist Amartya Sen, included everything from having a proper resistance to disease to having the ability to realize one's talents. To enable citizens to fulfil these capabilities as much as possible, he argued, we needed to rethink our attitude to both economics and politics (Norman 2010: 129–30). Economically, he believed we should celebrate competition and entrepreneurship but also recognize that they have their limitations, acknowledging that economic competition will only work well in the context of having appropriate institutions, and that in certain circumstances limiting competition and encouraging co-ops will be more beneficial (Norman 2010: 166–9). Politically, Norman argued, it was imperative that we reject the combination of libertarianism and centralized control that had characterized

Thatcherism in practice, and re-emphasize instead the importance of intermediate institutions, in a tradition that he attempted to trace all the way back to Aristotle (Norman 2010: 212–15).

There was of course scope to doubt whether Norman's practical prescriptions to realize such ideals – which included re-empowering local councils, simplifying the tax system and reforming corporate governance – were really radical enough to live up to the grandness of his theory. But certainly in intention, his position was designed to mark a distinct break from parts of the New Right – at least insofar as it had embraced what Gray had labelled 'free-market fundamentalism'.

Conservative Response IV: Neo-conservatism

If one reaction to the challenges that confronted conservatives in the 1970s and 1980s was 'traditionalism', another that proved influential, particularly in the United States, was a movement usually known as 'neo-conservatism'. Summarizing the tenets of neo-conservatism is a difficult task, since it included a fairly disparate array of thinkers – including, perhaps most influentially, the founder of the Cold War magazine *Encounter*, Irving Kristol; the writer and commentator Norman Podhoretz; and Jeanne Kirkpatrick, President Reagan's ambassador to the United Nations. Moreover, these figures were influenced by a wide variety of intellectual sources, including evangelical Christianity and Leo Strauss's commitment to natural law, as well as – to a lesser extent – by a conventional New Right belief that an over-large welfare state can stifle individual self-responsibility and initiative. However, broadly speaking, one can define neo-conservatism by its adherence to three main ideological positions.

First, the most important aspect of neo-conservatism was its approach to foreign policy. This was originally inspired by the circumstances of the Cold War, and in particular by the neo-conservatives' distaste for American administrations pursuing accommodation with the USSR, as opposed to its direct overthrow, in the 1960s and 1970s. Instead, the neo-conservatives argued, in line with Kirkpatrick's influential essay 'Dictatorships and Double Standards' (1979), that the Soviet Union should be confronted more directly, eschewing the dishonourable compromises of détente, and reasserting the role of the United States as the leader of the free world after the humiliation of the Vietnam War. Crucially, Kirkpatrick argued, it was essential to distinguish between revolutionary communist regimes that attempt to control and rework every aspect of society, and more traditional autocracies, which do not seek to disrupt the normal rhythms of life – with the latter definitely to be preferred to the former (Hoeveler 1991: 159–60). So, where possible, the neo-conservatives maintained, democracy should be encouraged. Indeed, by the time of President George W. Bush's administration, neo-conservatism in the hands of Vice President Dick Cheney, Defence Secretary Donald Rumsfeld and Deputy Defence Secretary Paul Wolfowitz became synonymous with the attempt to foster democracy in the Middle East, most notably in Iraq. But in fact the core of the neo-conservative case was that democracy should only be introduced where this was possible; where it was not, autocracies should be supported against the threat of communism, as being vastly preferable ideologically.

Second, following on from this hard-headed approach to foreign affairs, neo-conservatives were cautious supporters of free-market capitalism. While they accepted the main thrust of the New Right case that an over-extensive welfare state could act as a disincentive to hard work, like the traditionalists they worried that unregulated capitalism leads not simply to greater prosperity and opportunity for all, but rather to serious inequality, class conflict and political instability. In such circumstances, neo-conservatives like Kristol argued, capitalism deserves only 'two cheers', and an inheritance tax, a graduated income tax and a basic welfare state were thus essential for a civilized modern state. Finally, despite their strong opposition to the permissive values of the 1960s, the neo-conservatives were only qualified admirers of religion. They accepted its worth in fostering a strong sense of morality, but also worried that at its worst it simply led to greater intolerance and fanaticism. As such, they tended to be strong defenders of the separation of church and state, and thus were distinct from the 'moral majority' wing of the American New Right.

Conservative Response V: Conservative Populism – Saviour or Cuckoo?

The final type of conservatism we should consider, which has become a significant feature of European and American politics in the twenty-first century, and perhaps particularly since the global financial crash of 2007–8, is 'populist conservatism'. This is a controversial topic, partly because 'populism' is so difficult to define, but also because both political thinkers and politicians have disagreed over how compatible populism and conservatism are. To some extent, if populism is simply defined as vigorously seeking to uphold the interests of 'ordinary people' against a corrupt 'elite' or 'establishment', then it is hardly a new phenomenon. Thus, in the United States in the nineteenth century, the term was loosely applied to President Andrew Jackson with his campaign against a 'corrupt aristocracy' on behalf of the 'common man'; at the turn of the twentieth century to the Democrat presidential candidate William Jennings Bryan with his campaign in favour of farmers against corporations; and more recently to the third-party candidature of George Wallace, the racist governor of Alabama, who campaigned in 1968 in favour of continued southern segregation. In Italy, just to take one European example, prime ministers Bettino Craxi in the 1980s and Silvio Berlusconi in the 1990s were often labelled 'populists', on the basis that they substituted showmanship for political ideology (Muller 2013b: 82). Furthermore, as mentioned already in this chapter, to some extent a populist element forms an intrinsic component of the American New Right. But given the much greater electoral success in the twenty-first century of 'populists' such as Donald Trump in the USA, Victor Orbán in Hungary, Nigel Farage's Brexit campaign in Britain, and to some extent Geert Wilders in the Netherlands and Beppe Grillo in Italy, the question of the relationship of populism to conservatism

– and indeed of how to define populism in the first place – has necessarily assumed more urgency.

Why, then, have some recent forms of populism been grouped together with conservatism? Essentially, there are four main reasons. First, populists are often deemed to be trying to manage historical change, but fearfully, even resentfully, appealing to groups of people 'left behind' by rapid socio-economic or cultural change, in a way not entirely dissimilar to conservatives' suspicion of revolutionary change. Hence Donald Trump's appeal in 2016 to industrial workers in the traditional 'rust belt' states of the Mid-West, such as Pennsylvania, Wisconsin and Michigan, whose jobs were threatened by rapid technological change.[10] Second, such populists often appeal to the importance of national tradition, or at least a traditional culture, in a way that appears similar to conservatives – who, as we have seen, are quite happy to invoke traditions that are more or less invented as well as those that are more genuine. An obvious example here is Trump's vague but successful slogan 'Make America Great Again'. But more generally, populists like Nigel Farage in Britain, or Jarosław Kaczyński in Poland, have appealed to an idealized version of their country's national past, usually emphasizing the socially conservative nature of it – often to the detriment of minority groups, such as individuals identifying as LGBT or people of colour (Taggart 2004). Third, on a related point, populists of this sort often combine a dedication to an idolized past with an aggressive nationalism, contrasting the authentic possessors of a national tradition with recent immigrants, particularly those who are culturally or ethnically in a minority. Hence Trump's demonization of Mexican immigrants as being drug dealers, criminals and likely to commit rape, or the scare stories during the Brexit referendum about the European Union being liable to let in endless Turkish immigrants, who could then migrate to Britain (Reilly 2016; Morris 2019). This is not by any means a position that has historically been shared by all conservatives, of course, but it has its unpleasant antecedents in, say, the anti-Dreyfusard writings of the 1890s that we examined in Chapter 3. Finally, a key part of populist rhetoric, contempt for politics, appears to have echoes within conservatism, which has traditionally been sceptical of the idea that political activity represents some kind of apogee of human achievement, as opposed to a vital but ultimately unfortunate necessity, stemming from humanity's imperfection. If populist rhetoric about the corruptness of politics is more vehement, the argument goes, nevertheless it has a very definite echo within a conservative tradition that has always sought to uphold other areas of human achievement as more important.

There are, however, five reasons to be sceptical about identifying populism with conservatism too closely. First, most obviously, it is difficult to *identify* populism with conservatism because there are demonstrably populist movements that have a radical rather than a conservative character. If this phenomenon is not common in Europe and the USA, it is much more so in Latin America, the Hugo Chávez government in Venezuela being a notable recent example. Second, most fundamentally, populists are much more intrinsically hostile to pluralism than conservatives are: if populists have one core belief, it is that the 'people' can be regarded as one indissoluble entity. As such, those hostile to a populist movement are often discounted as inauthentic or even 'unreal' – hence the claim by Nigel Farage that Brexit was a victory for 'the real people, for the ordinary people, for the decent people', as though somehow those who had opposed Brexit were not simply wrong, but not genuinely British citizens (Muller 2016: 19–22; Withnall 2016). By contrast, recent conservatives, even on the New Right, have been much more accepting of the idea of democratic difference and of pluralism; while they are certainly happy to portray their opponents' ideologies in an unfavourable light, this is not the same as suggesting that those advocating such ideologies are 'unreal'. Indeed, a common trope, as we have seen, is to excuse 'ordinary, decent' socialists for being misled, rather than to suggest they do not count as citizens at all.

Third, following on from this, conservatives have tended to be much more respectful of traditional political machinery and of historic civil society institutions. While Margaret Thatcher, for example, may have had some definite populist inclinations – even to the point of abolishing institutions she did not like, such as the Greater London Council – she was in general highly conservative constitutionally, laying great emphasis on a traditional conception of the 'rule of law'. By contrast, populists are much happier to assail traditional institutions that, according to them, are opposing the 'will of the people' – as evidenced by the hostility shown to judges and judicial decisions in Britain after the Brexit referendum, when they were deemed to be hindering or opposing Brexit. (It is worth noting, too, that this does not necessarily imply an unqualified love of referendums by populists: the referendum is to *confirm* the 'real' will of the people, not to *discover* it [Muller 2016: 29].) Fourth, populists tend to be much more willing to attack traditional elites than conservatives are: for the latter, managing change often means preserving or resuscitating traditional structures; for populists, being against the 'elite' or the 'establishment' is very much part of their core message. For this reason, lack of sophistication or taste is often presented as the very badge of authenticity – despite his enormous wealth, Donald Trump exhibits his identity with 'real' people by preferring fast food and 'bad-taste' opulence (Midgette 2016). Finally, populism, partly as a consequence of its ideological lightness, and of its conviction that the will of the people is genuinely unitary, is relaxed about ideological contradictions in a way that conservatism is not.[11] The Brexit campaign was a case in point. Was Brexit designed to protect the forgotten workers of a rapidly deindustrializing Britain, pulling up the drawbridge to prevent unfair foreign competition? Or was it designed to release the country from the shackles of over-regulation by the European Union, so that Britain could become a genuinely free-market economy, with fewer protections for workers and a more ruthlessly competitive culture?[12] The answer remains unclear. Whatever overlaps there are between conservatism and (right-wing) populism, in other words, they remain ideologically highly distinct beasts.

Conclusion

In summary, the advent of the New Right in the 1970s and 1980s presented conservatives with many new opportunities, but also some novel challenges. As we have seen, the end of the economic 'golden age' in 1973, and the associated collapse in the hegemony of Keynesianism, offered conservatives in Britain and the United States considerable new opportunities, both theoretically and practically. Hence the popularity of Thatcherism and Reaganism, which combined a commitment to the free market with a renewed defence of the nation and the traditional family – in part to counter the rise of the 'permissive' values of the 1960s. However, as we also saw, by the 1990s and 2000s, concerns about how Thatcherism and Reaganism had operated in practice led some conservatives to worry about the degree of centralization that New Right conservatism had enabled, and whether it was in fact itself undermining traditional values. Finally, we briefly examined conservatism's ambivalent relationship with populism, emphatically rejecting the idea that the two are identical, albeit that there is sometimes an ideological overlap in practice.

Epilogue

Predicting the future for any political ideology is no easy task, to say the least. Few political thinkers or politicians in the middle of the nineteenth century, for example, would have predicted quite how important Marxist socialism was going to be in the twentieth. Equally, few in the middle of the twentieth century would have guessed how relatively quickly the Eastern bloc was going to collapse. Conversely, few mid-nineteenth-century thinkers would have guessed how embattled theories of political economy and classical liberalism were to become by 1900, let alone predicted their resurgence in the last quarter of the twentieth century. Such difficulties are compounded in the case of conservatism by the fact that it is a fundamentally reactive ideology, one that generally seeks to manage change cautiously, while transforming opposing ideologies' concepts to its own advantage. As such, trying to draw firm conclusions about the directions conservatism is likely to take in the future – even if they are based on (for example) plausible speculations about the environment, the geopolitical ambitions of China, or the impact of the internet on global politics – is at best a highly speculative activity.

What we can reasonably conclude from the survey of conservative thought contained in this volume is that prophecies concerning the demise of conservatism are much more likely to appear in the near future than the event itself.

Theorists in the 1950s, like Daniel Bell, spoke of 'the end of ideology', on the basis that welfare-state capitalism had 'solved' many of the problems in Western democracies; after the fall of communism in the late 1980s, politicians and political thinkers in the 1990s briefly hailed the triumph of liberalism and a 'new world order', implying the demise of other political ideologies. But both diagnoses were proved false. Welfare-state capitalism became much more embattled in the 1970s after the end of the economic 'golden age', while the optimism of the 1990s ran head-first into the shock of 11 September 2001, and the renewed global ambitions of Russia. More specifically, historians and theorists like John Weiss and John Gray have periodically predicted the end of the viability of conservatism – the former on the basis that traditional elites had been eliminated by 1945, and the latter on the basis that the global capitalism of the 1980s and 1990s had eliminated the kind of local knowledge that had previously made conservatism possible (Weiss 1977: 174; Gray 1997b: 38–46). But these diagnoses, too, have proved to be premature: conservatism found ways to adapt to new circumstances after the Second World War, and the effect of markets on local traditions has not, as yet, rendered conservatism obsolete. The formula of managing change cautiously, arguing that human conduct is best understood as part of an 'extra-human' order, and providing symbiotic opposites to progressive concepts in order to rebut them, has proved extremely durable. Conservatism, at least for the foreseeable future, is here to stay.

Notes

Chapter 1

1 For just one example, see Nisbet 1986: 21–74; see also Freeden 1996: 331–2.

2 Ironically, Huntington did not in fact himself remain loyal to his definition of conservatism as essentially reactive, also claiming that 'the essence of conservatism can be summed up in a small number of basic ideas' (Huntington 1957: 457).

3 See below, Chapters 2 and 5, and Gray 1997a.

4 See below, Chapter 2.

5 It is true that to some extent Oakeshott and Gilmour both admitted that a conservative approach to tradition was more complex than this. Oakeshott, in particular, especially in his later work, emphasized that a tradition is not a monolithic entity, but instead composed of a set of diverse practices (see, for example, Oakeshott 1975: 55–60 and Oakeshott 1976). This did not, however, dislodge Oakeshott from his fundamental conviction that there is a dominant tendency within the Western European tradition favouring individualism. As such, he believed those opposing it were not merely in *disagreement*, but *mistaken* (Oakeshott 1991: 363–83).

6 See Mannheim: 'the conservative mode of experience thus preserves itself ... by raising to the level of reflection and methodical control those attitudes to the world which would otherwise have been lost to authentic experience' (1986: 101).

7 Although conservatism apparently advocates a huge variety of different positions, Freeden argues that as an ideology it

does much more than simply provide a knee-jerk reaction to progressive ideologies at any given moment, as Huntington would contend. Rather, while it deploys political concepts more eclectically than progressive ideologies do, it does not do so in a *purely* reactive manner, but instead seeks to establish counter-progressive positions which may have considerable potential to endure.

8 Compare, by contrast, the approach taken by Eatwell and O'Sullivan (1989) on 'the nature of the Right'.

9 It should be emphasized that I am definitely *not* implying that conservatism is a uniquely Western phenomenon – the idea that historical change should be managed cautiously, that human limitations should be accepted, and that human actions are subject to an 'extra-human' force, can be found in a number of non-Western traditions of thought, including, for example, Confucianism. Moreover, at least some Western thinkers have been well aware of this. Despite often being regarded as a 'quintessentially English' conservative thinker, Oakeshott in fact gives a number of Confucian examples to illustrate his arguments, particularly in the essays collected in *Rationalism in Politics* (see Oakeshott 1991: 41 n. 41, 236 n. 8, 480 n. 2).

10 In Chapter 2, I consider Britain, France and the United States separately, while Chapters 3, 4 and 5 unfold more thematically. There are obviously arguments for and against such a structure but the greater interconnectedness of the world after the mid-nineteenth century gives it at least some plausibility.

Chapter 2

1 The changes that occurred within 'natural philosophy' in the seventeenth century were of course immensely complex, and resist easy summary – not least because Newton himself reintroduced questions concerning 'attractive forces' that earlier seventeenth-century thinkers had thought settled. There were also notable questions about chemistry and biology that remained unresolved by 1800. But there is no doubt that Newton was enormously influential on Enlightenment thinkers. For good accounts of seventeenth-century scientific developments, see Dear 2009 and Koyré 1957; for Newton, see Westfall 1980.

2 For just one influential book on this highly complex debate, see Furet 1981.

3 This too was a complex debate. Scottish Enlightenment thinkers, such as David Hume and Adam Smith, were generally optimistic

that greater commerce would encourage more 'politeness' and decorum within society. Others, by contrast, followed the earlier eighteenth-century thinker Andrew Fletcher in worrying that greater commercial activity undermined military virtue by encouraging landowners to renege on their military obligations and to accede to a standing army instead, funded by taxes on their estates, thereby encouraging political corruption and indolence. Others again were attracted by the arguments of the early eighteenth-century thinker Bernard Mandeville – namely that greater commercial activity brought public benefits, but only at the cost of encouraging private vices – while some followed Francis Hutcheson in arguing that the human ability to behave morally was innate. For ways into these debates, see Pocock 1985; Porter and Teich 1981; Hont and Ignatieff 1983.

4 Since voting was organized around parishes and ancient pieces of property, many new city dwellers lacked the vote.

5 This fact has made some scholars wary of labelling Burke a 'conservative' at all, and certainly his thought was subsequently reinterpreted and repackaged much more explicitly (see Jones 2017). But of course the constituent parts of a concept or ideology can be present without the word being used, as John Gunnell amongst others has insisted (Gunnell 1998). More substantively, Richard Bourke has argued that it is a mistake to regard Burke as opposed to abstract, Enlightenment reasoning, seeing him rather as a thinker who continued to embrace Lockean doctrines of resistance and as an upholder of abstract rights. This is an important interpretation, but it is not one that has been universally accepted, and it sits uneasily with some of the passages in Burke's *Reflections* cited here (Bourke 2015). For a sophisticated exploration of Burke as a 'conservative', see Hampsher-Monk 2015.

6 By the eighteenth century, it had become clear that one could not plausibly trace back such an inheritance to an original 'ancient constitution'. But, Burke maintained, this was relatively unimportant – the critical point was that a 'powerful prepossession towards antiquity' continued to exist amongst lawyers in particular, and the public more generally (Burke 1968: 118).

7 In particular, Burke maintained that the Glorious Revolution of 1688 had not established any precedent for removing rulers who failed to uphold certain liberties and property rights (Burke 1968: 101).

8 It is true that Burke does talk in *Reflections* of society being a contract between the dead, the living and the yet to be born. But this significantly transforms the idea of a 'contract' away from its Lockean origins.

9 Unlike Scottish Enlightenment thinkers such as Hume and Smith, therefore, who argued that the market itself tended to encourage men to become more civil, rational and refined, and hence better able to operate in the market, Burke maintained that the market's 'alchemical' power to transform even the most solid and traditional phenomena into something provisional and unstable necessarily threatens to undermine the very conditions that make it possible (Burke 1968: 359, 369).

10 This hostility to reform of any kind in fact proved increasingly difficult to uphold as the 1820s proceeded, in view of the understandable demands for Catholic emancipation in the wake of union with Ireland in 1801, which ultimately led to splits within the Tory Party.

11 It is worth noting that all of these figures had originally been radical supporters of the French Revolution. For a useful introduction to them, see Morrow 2011.

12 In fact, even within the economic sphere itself, they argued, the market did not behave as beneficently as Smith had claimed it would in *The Wealth of Nations*. For, rather than distributing goods more efficiently, and spreading profits more equitably and productively, as Smith had predicted, the result of increased market competition had in fact been the over-production of 'cheap and flimsy' goods and an increase in unproductive wealth, unequally distributed (Southey 1829: II, 247–55; 1832: I, 193–6).

13 The revolution not only changed political arrangements fundamentally, but also the calendar and currency, weights and measures, and places and street names (see Jennings 2011: 2).

14 Mallet du Pan, however, was much less convinced than Burke of the importance of intervening 'civil society' bodies between individual and state.

15 One particularly famous contribution to this debate was made by Benjamin Constant, who claimed that a key problem of the revolution was that it had misunderstood the nature of liberty in a modern commercial society – so that it had elevated public life over private enjoyments and preferences in a way inapplicable to modern life. See Constant 1980: 172–5.

16 It should be stressed that, in saying this, I do not intend to imply that the founding fathers were 'pro-slavery' in any simple sense, or that the constitution was designed to uphold slavery as a principle. Rather, the three-fifths clause should be seen as a compromise between the incompatible claims of slave-holding and non-slave-holding states. Slave states originally wanted their representation in Congress to be proportional to their financial contributions, and, when this became unworkable,

to the size of their populations, as proxy for this. The clause, therefore, was as much designed to *reduce* the influence of slave states as it was to legitimize slavery. Nevertheless, it remains the case that tolerating slavery as an institution sat uneasily with Enlightenment principles of equality – a fact which many founding fathers themselves felt acutely. For a good account of the clause and the circumstances and issues surrounding it, see Beeman 2009, chapter 11, especially 268–71.

17 Furthermore, even those who were strongly critical of slavery, such as Lincoln, argued that there were groups (like native Americans and Mexicans) who were 'dependent by nature', and hence unfit to take advantage of the opportunities afforded by land ownership. On this basis, they sought to undermine the rights of native Americans and Mexicans to their lands (Foner 1995: xxvii).

Chapter 3

1 Mallock did not of course believe that democratic government would 'represent' the masses in a democracy; rather, he believed that the masses could be effectively manipulated – albeit that such manipulation would be in the masses' real best interests. As such, his position bears comparison with that of the Italian sociologist Vilfredo Pareto. See below, Chapter 4.

2 It should be noted that Spencer thought that aspects of more primitive homogeneous societies and more sophisticated heterogeneous societies could exist simultaneously – and that the progression from more homogeneous to more heterogeneous ones was far from unilinear and simple. As he put it: evolution implied no 'uniform ascent from lower to higher', because the cosmic process brought 'retrogression as well as progression' (Spencer 1876–96: III, 599).

3 Furthermore, the Supreme Court in those years proved to be a powerful supporter of capitalism in the later nineteenth century, using the 'due process' clause of the 14th Amendment to the constitution, passed after the end of the Civil War (Young 2018: 134–5).

Chapter 4

1 It is notable that Baldwin stressed the importance of 'England', not 'Britain'.

2 This argument is of course based on the further premise that 'technical' knowledge represents only an abstract and inferior

form of practical knowledge, rather than a form of knowledge to be valued in its own right. This underpins Oakeshott's typically conservative suspicion of 'abstract' political ideologies.

3   It is true that Oakeshott did warn there are citizens in society scared of embracing the possibilities offered by genuine individualism, and who sought 'solidarity' and 'equality' by way of alternatives. Mass society thus presents dangers as well as opportunities; hence Oakeshott's conservative caution (see Oakeshott 1991: 372–81).

4   This description of liberalism is a classic example of a conservative unfairly stereotyping an opposing ideology.

Chapter 5

1   The degree to which welfare states in Western societies expanded in the 1960s varied considerably, of course, but President Lyndon Johnson's ambition to build a 'Great Society' in the United States, and the expansion of welfare services in Britain under Harold Wilson's 1964–70 administration (partly in response to 'the rediscovery of poverty' in the early 1960s by social scientists), both represented important developments.

2   This is not to imply that charting the fortunes of conservatism in Western and Eastern Europe after the 1960s is not a fascinating study. Examining, for example, how the French Right evolved into Gaullist, centrist and Front National variants would be extremely interesting. Equally, there is little doubt that the most important and influential versions of conservative ideology in this period were those of the Anglo-American New Right.

3   It is true that Hayek, unlike many conservatives, sought rational justification for the principles provided to us by social evolution. But even granting this, the role of reason remained very limited compared to that envisaged by most progressive liberals (Freeden 1996: 307).

4   The late judge Antonin Scalia, appointed by President Reagan, was one notable example, but there have been a number of others.

5   In view of one of Powell's allusions, the speech is known almost universally as the 'Rivers of Blood' speech.

6   Not for nothing did Goldwater claim that the USA would be 'better off if we could just saw off the eastern seaboard and let it float out to sea', contrasting the corrupt East with a free West where every day 'individual initiative made the desert bloom' (Micklethwait and Wooldridge 2004: 58).

7   It should be noted that such traditionalist conservatives generally

approved of reducing government interference in market transactions, and of upholding the importance of private property
rights, more than post-war social democrats had done. But this
was a much more minor part of their programme than it was
for the Thatcherites.

8 Scruton claimed to derive this conclusion from his reading of
Hegel, but of course this is not the only conclusion one might
draw from Hegel's view of the relationship of individual and
state, and some Hegel scholars would strongly dispute Scruton's
conservative reading.

9 To pick just one particularly influential example: the Harvard
academic Louis Hartz argued in *The Liberal Tradition in
America* (1955) that the lack of a feudal aristocracy and a class-
conscious working class meant that the USA was a purely liberal
society. As we have seen in previous chapters, this is a highly
controversial claim, but it was a popular position amongst
American political scientists in the 1950s and 1960s.

10 See Muller 2016: 16–17. Muller cautions against 'explaining
away' such grievances too readily, on the basis that this
reveals an unstated theoretical commitment to a certain type of
modernization.

11 As has been stressed, conservatives often end up in very different
groupings that are inconsistent with one another. But any given
conservative group's arguments usually have internal coherence.
The same is emphatically not true of populists.

12 I owe the point about Brexit to Professor Colin Hay (Sciences
Po).

Bibliography

Acomb, F. (1973) *Mallet du Pan: A Career in Political Journalism.* Durham, NC: Duke University Press.

Adams, C. F. (ed.) (1850–6) *The Works of John Adams.* 10 vols. Boston, MA: Little and Brown.

Adams, H. (1918) *The Education of Henry Adams*, ed. H. C. Lodge. Boston, MA: Houghton Mifflin.

Agresto, J. (2003) 'John C. Calhoun and the Re-examination of American Democracy', in B.-P. Frost and J. Sikkenga, eds., *History of American Political Thought.* Lanham, MD: Lexington Books, pp. 316–24.

Bairoch, P. (1978) 'Citta/Campagna', in *Enciclopedia Einaudi 3.* Turin, pp. 85–106.

Baldwin, S. (1923) 'Speech at Manchester', *The Times*, 3 November.

Baldwin, S. (1926) *On England and Other Essays.* London: Philip Allan and Co.

Barrès, M. (1906) *Scènes et Doctrines du Nationalisme.* Paris: F. Juven.

Bayley, C. and Biagini, E. (2008) 'Introduction – Giuseppe Mazzini's International Political Thought', in C. Bayley and E. Biagini, eds., *Giuseppe Mazzini and the Globalization of Democratic Nationalism, 1830–1920.* Oxford: Oxford University Press.

Beeman, R. (2009) *Plain, Honest, Men: The Making of the American Constitution.* New York: Random House.

Bell, D. (2000) *The End of Ideology.* Cambridge, MA: Harvard University Press.

Bellamy, R. (2003) 'The Advent of the Masses and the Making of the Modern Theory of Democracy', in T. Ball and R. Bellamy, eds., *The Cambridge History of Twentieth-Century Political Thought*. Cambridge: Cambridge University Press, pp. 70–103.

Bentham, J. (1973) 'Political Principles', in B. Parekh, ed., *Bentham's Political Thought*. London: Croom Helm, pp. 295–308.

Berend, I. (2014) 'A Restructured Economy: From the Oil Crisis to the Financial Crisis, 1973–2009', in D. Stone, ed., *The Oxford Handbook of Postwar European History*. Oxford: Oxford University Press, pp. 406–22.

Berlin, I. (1994) 'Introduction', in R. Lebrun, ed. and trans., *Joseph de Maistre: Considerations on France*. Cambridge: Cambridge University Press, pp. xi–xxxiv.

Bernstein, E. (1961) *Evolutionary Socialism: A Criticism and Affirmation*, trans. E. C. Harvey. New York: Schocken Books.

Biddiss, M. D. (1970) *Father of Racist Ideology: The Social and Political Thought of Count Gobineau*. London: Weidenfeld and Nicolson.

Black, E. and Black, M. (2002) *The Rise of the Southern Republicans*. Cambridge, MA: Belknap Press.

Black, L. (2003) *The Political Culture of the Left in Affluent Britain, 1951–1964: Old Labour, New Britain?* Basingstoke: Palgrave Macmillan.

Blinkhorn, M. (2011) 'The Fascist Challenge', in G. Martel, ed., *A Companion to Europe, 1900–1945*. Oxford: Blackwell, pp. 309–25.

Bonald, L. G. A. (1859) *Œuvres Complètes*. 3 vols. Paris: J-P. Migne.

Bourke, R. (2015) *Empire and Revolution: The Political Life of Edmund Burke*. Princeton, NJ: Princeton University Press.

Bourke, R. (2018) 'What Is Conservatism?', *European Journal of Political Theory*, 17(4), pp. 449–75.

Bradley, J. L. and Ousby, I. (eds.) (1987) *The Correspondence of John Ruskin and Charles Eliot Norton*. Cambridge: Cambridge University Press.

Brown, C. (2001) *The Death of Christian Britain*. London: Routledge.

Brunetière, F. (1899) *Les Ennemis de L'Ame Française*. Paris: J. Hetzel.

Buckley, W. (1959) *Up from Liberalism*. New York: McDowell.

Burke, E. (1889) *The Works of the Right Honourable Edmund Burke*. 8 vols. Bohn Library Edition. London: George Bell and Sons.

Burke, E. (1968) *Reflections on the Revolution in France*. Harmondsworth: Penguin.

Cahm, E. (1996) *The Dreyfus Affair in French Politics and Society*. London: Longman.

Calhoun, J. C. (1953) *A Disquisition on Government, and Selections from the Discourse.* Indianapolis, IN: Bobbs-Merrill Co.

Carlyle, T. (1893) *Critical and Miscellaneous Essays.* 8 vols. London: Chapman and Hall.

Cecil, H. (1908) 'Presidential Address', in H. M. Judge, ed., *Political Socialism: A Remonstrance.* London: P. S. King and Son.

Cecil, H. (1910) *Liberty and Authority.* London: Edward Arnold.

Cecil, H. (1912) *Conservatism.* London: Williams and Norgate.

Chase, W. J. (2011) 'The Socialist Experiment', in G. Martel, ed., *A Companion to Europe, 1900–1945.* Oxford: Blackwell, pp. 292–308.

Chateaubriand, F.-R. (1861) *Œuvres Complètes.* 12 vols. Paris: Garnier.

Chateaubriand, F.-R. (1966) *Le Génie du Christianisme.* 2 vols. Paris: Garnier-Flammarion.

Coleridge, S. T. (1969) *The Collected Works of Samuel Taylor Coleridge*, ed. K. Coburn et al. 15 vols. Princeton, NJ: Princeton University Press.

Collini, S. (2000) 'The European Modernist as Anglican Moralist: The Later Social Criticism of T. S. Eliot', in M. S. Micale and R. L. Diettle, eds., *Enlightenment, Passion, Modernity.* Stanford, CA: Stanford University Press, pp. 207–29.

The Conservative Manifesto (1979) London: Conservative Central Office.

The Conservative Manifesto: The Next Moves Forward (1987) London: Conservative Central Office.

Constant, B. (1980) 'De la Liberté chez les Modernes', in M. Gauchet, ed., *De la Liberté Chez les Modernes: Ecrits Politiques.* Paris: Librairie Générale Française.

Crafts, N. and Toniolo, G. (2014) '"*Les Trente Glorieuses*": From the Marshall Plan to the Oil Crisis', in D. Stone, ed., *The Oxford Handbook to Postwar European History.* Oxford: Oxford University Press, pp. 356–78.

Darcel, J.-L. (1988) 'Maistre and the French Revolution', in R. Lebrun, ed., *Maistre Studies.* Lanham, MD: University Press of America.

Dear, P. (2009) *Revolutionizing the Sciences: European Knowledge and Its Ambitions, 1500–1700.* Princeton, NJ: Princeton University Press.

Dorey, P. (2011) *British Conservatism: The Politics and Philosophy of Inequality.* London: I. B. Tauris.

Dorpalen, A. (1957) *Heinrich von Treitschke.* New Haven, CT: Yale University Press.

Draus, F. (1989) 'Burke et les Français', in F. Furet and M. Ozouf, eds., *The Transformation of Political Culture, 1789–1848*. Oxford: Pergamon, pp. 79–99.

Easton, D. (1953) *The Political System*. New York: Knopf.

Eastwood, D. (1989) 'Robert Southey and the Intellectual Origins of Romantic Conservatism', *English Historical Review*, 104(411), pp. 308–31.

Eatwell, R. (1996) 'On Defining the "Fascist Minimum"': The Centrality of Ideology', *Journal of Political Ideologies*, 1(3), pp. 303–19.

Eatwell, R. and O'Sullivan, N. (eds.) (1989) *The Nature of the Right*. London: Pinter.

Eccleshall, R. (ed.) (1990) *English Conservatism since the Restoration*. London: Unwin Hyman.

Eichengreen, B. (2007) *The European Economy since 1945: Coordinated Capitalism and Beyond*. Princeton, NJ: Princeton University Press.

Eley, G. (1983) 'What Produces Fascism? Preindustrial Traditions or a Crisis of the Capitalist State', *Politics and Society*, 12(1), pp. 53–82.

Eley, G. (2014) 'Corporatism and the Social Democratic Moment: The Postwar Settlement, 1945–73', in D. Stone, ed., *The Oxford Handbook of Postwar European History*. Oxford: Oxford University Press, pp. 37–59.

Eliot, T. S. (1939) *The Idea of a Christian Society*. London: Faber.

Eliot, T. S. (1948) *Notes Towards the Definition of Culture*. London: Faber.

Evans, E. (1997) *Thatcher and Thatcherism*. London: Routledge.

Evans, R. J. W. and von Strandmann, H. P. (eds.) (2000) *The Revolutions in Europe 1848–1849: From Reform to Reaction*. Oxford: Oxford University Press.

Farrall, S. and Jennings, W. (2014) 'Thatcherism and Crime: The Beast that Never Roared?', in S. Farrall and C. Hay, eds., *The Legacy of Thatcherism*. Oxford: Oxford University Press/British Academy, pp. 207–33.

Fitzhugh, G. (1854) *Sociology for the South: or, the Failure of Free Society*. Richmond, VA: A. Morris.

Fitzhugh, G. (1960) *Cannibals All, or Slaves without Masters*, ed. C. Vann Woodward. Cambridge, MA: Harvard University Press.

Foner, E. (1995) *Free Soil, Free Labour, Free Men: The Ideology of the Republican Party before the Civil War*. New York: Oxford University Press.

Ford, D. J. (1974) 'W. H. Mallock and Socialism in England', in K. D. Brown, ed., *Essays in Anti-Labour History*. London: Macmillan, pp. 317–42.

Francis, M. and Morrow, J. (1994) *A History of English Political Thought in the Nineteenth Century*. London: Duckworth.

Freeden, M. (1996) *Ideologies and Political Theory: A Conceptual Approach*. Oxford: Clarendon Press.

Furet, F. (1981) *Interpreting the French Revolution*. Cambridge: Cambridge University Press.

Gamble, A. (1994) *The Free Economy and the Strong State*. Basingstoke: Macmillan.

Garrard, J. (2006) 'The Democratic Experience', in S. Berger, ed., *A Companion to Nineteenth-Century Europe, 1789–1914*. Oxford: Blackwell, pp. 149–63.

Gassert, P. (2014) 'The Spectre of Americanization: Western Europe in the American Century', in D. Stone, ed., *The Oxford Handbook of Postwar European History*. Oxford: Oxford University Press, pp. 182–200.

Geppert, A. C. T. (2010) *Fleeting Cities: Imperial Expositions in Fin-de-Siècle Europe*. Basingstoke: Palgrave Macmillan.

Gerwarth, R. (2017) *The Vanquished: Why the First World War Failed to End*. London: Penguin.

Gildea, R. (1996) *France, 1870–1914*. London: Longman.

Gilmour, I. (1977) *Inside Right: A Study of Conservatism*. London: Hutchinson.

Godechot, J. (1971) *The Counter-revolution: Doctrine and Action, 1789–1804*, trans. S. Attanasio, New York: Howard Fertig.

Goldman, L. (2011) 'Conservative Political Thought from the Revolutions of 1848 until the *Fin de Siècle*', in G. Stedman Jones and G. Claeys, eds., *The Cambridge History of Nineteenth-Century Political Thought*. Cambridge: Cambridge University Press, pp. 691–719.

Gray, J. (1984) *Hayek on Liberty*. Oxford: Blackwell.

Gray, J. (1993) *Beyond the New Right*. London: Routledge.

Gray, J. (1997a) *Enlightenment's Wake*. London: Routledge.

Gray, J. (1997b) 'The Undoing of Conservatism', in J. Gray and D. Willetts, *Is Conservatism Dead?* London: Profile Books, pp. 3–65.

Green, E. H. H. (1999) 'Thatcherism: An Historical Perspective', *Transactions of the Royal Historical Society*, 9, pp. 17–42.

Green, E. H. H. (2002) *Ideologies of Conservatism*. Oxford: Oxford University Press.

Greenleaf, W. H. (1983–7) *The British Political Tradition*. 3 vols. London: Routledge (I and III); London: Methuen (II).

Grimley, M. (2012) 'Thatcherism, Morality, and Religion', in B. Jackson and R. Saunders, eds., *Making Thatcher's Britain*. Cambridge: Cambridge University Press, pp. 78–94.

Gunnell, J. G. (1998) 'Time and Interpretation: Understanding Concepts and Conceptual Change', *History of Political Thought*, 19(4), pp. 641–58.

Haeckel, E. (1876) *The History of Creation, or the Development of the Earth and Its Inhabitants by the Action of Natural Causes*, trans. E. R. Lankester. 2 vols. London: Kegan Paul.

Hampsher-Monk, I. (2015) 'Edmund Burke in the Tory World', in J. Black, ed., *The Tory World: Deep History and the Tory Theme in British Foreign Policy, 1679–2014*. Aldershot: Ashgate, pp. 83–103.

Hanhimaki, J. M. (2014) 'Europe's Cold War', in D. Stone, ed., *The Oxford Handbook of Postwar European History*. Oxford: Oxford University Press, pp. 283–98.

Hannah, L. (2004) 'A Failed Experiment: The State Ownership of Industry', in R. Floud and P. Johnson, eds., *The Cambridge Economic History of Modern Britain*. Cambridge: Cambridge University Press

Hansard (1831) HC Deb. Vol. 3 cols. 1673, 1821, 19 and 22 April.

Hartz, L. (1955) *The Liberal Tradition in America*. New York: Harcourt Brace.

Hayek, F. A. (1960) *The Constitution of Liberty*. London: Routledge and Kegan Paul.

Heffernan, R. (2000) *New Labour and Thatcherism*. Basingstoke: Macmillan.

Hernstein, R. and Murray, C. (1994) *The Bell Curve: Intelligence and Class Structure in American Life*. New York: Simon and Schuster.

Hilton, B. (1988) *The Age of Atonement: The Influence of Evangelicalism on Social and Economic Thought, 1785–1865*. Oxford: Oxford University Press.

Hobhouse, L. T. (1911) *Liberalism*. London: Oxford University Press.

Hobsbawm, E. (1987) *The Age of Empire, 1875–1914*. London: Weidenfeld and Nicolson.

Hobson, J. A. (1974) *The Crisis of Liberalism*, ed. P. F. Clarke. Hassocks: Harvester.

Hoeveler, J. D. (1991) *Watch on the Right: Conservative Intellectuals in the Reagan Era*. Madison: University of Wisconsin Press.

Hont, I. and Ignatieff, M. (eds.) (1983) *Wealth and Virtue: The Shaping of Political Economy in the Scottish Enlightenment*. Cambridge: Cambridge University Press.

Hoover, K. and Plant, R. (2015) *Conservative Capitalism in Britain and the United States: A Critical Appraisal*. London: Routledge.

Hume, D. (1965) *A Treatise of Human Nature*, ed. L. A. Selby-Bigge. Oxford: Clarendon Press.

Hume, D. (1985) *Essays, Moral, Political, and Literary*. Indianapolis, IN: Liberty Fund.

Huntington, S. (1957) 'Conservatism as an Ideology', *American Political Science Review*, 51(2), pp. 454–73.

Hutber, P. (1977) *The Decline and Fall of the Middle Class*. Harmondsworth: Penguin.

Jarvis, M. (2005) *Conservative Governments, Morality and Social Change in Affluent Britain*. Manchester: Manchester University Press.

Jennings, J. (2011) *Revolution and the Republic: A History of Political Thought in France since the Eighteenth Century*. Oxford: Oxford University Press.

Jones, E. (2017) *Edmund Burke and the Invention of Modern Conservatism, 1830–1914*. Oxford: Oxford University Press.

Kant, I. (1997) *Critique of Pure Reason*, ed. and trans. P. Guyer and A. Wood. Cambridge: Cambridge University Press.

Kirk, R. (2008) *The Conservative Mind*. New York: Barnes and Noble.

Klinck, D. (1996) *The French Counter-revolutionary Theorist, Louis de Bonald (1754–1840)*. New York: Peter Lang.

Koselleck, R. (2004) *Futures Past*, trans. K. Tribe. New York: Columbia University Press.

Koyré, A. (1957) *From the Closed World to the Infinite Universe*. Baltimore, MD: Johns Hopkins University Press.

Lambert, P. (2020) 'The Professionalization and Institutionalization of History', in S. Berger, H. Feldner and K. Passmore, eds., *Writing History: Theory and Practice*. London: Bloomsbury, pp. 43–62.

La Mettrie, J. O. de (1996) *Machine Man and Other Writings*, trans. A. Thomson. Cambridge: Cambridge University Press.

Lasswell, H. and Kaplan, A. (1950) *Power and Society*. New Haven, CT: Yale University Press.

Lebrun, R. (1965) *Throne and Altar: The Political and Religious Thought of Joseph de Maistre*. Ottawa: University of Ottawa Press.

Lee, R. (2006) 'Industrial Revolution, Commerce, and Trade', in S. Berger, ed., *A Companion to Nineteenth-Century Europe, 1789–1914*. Oxford: Blackwell, pp. 44–55.

Leonhard, J. (2006) 'The Rise of the Modern Leviathan', in S. Berger, ed., *A Companion to Nineteenth-Century Europe, 1789–1914*. Oxford: Blackwell, pp. 137–48.

Letwin, S. R. (1992) *The Anatomy of Thatcherism*. London: Fontana.

Lewis, W. A. (1978) *Growth and Fluctuations, 1870–1913*. London: Allen and Unwin.

Lipset, S. M. (1960) *Political Man*. London: Mercury Books.

McAleer, J. and MacKenzie, J. M. (eds.) (2015) *Exhibiting the Empire*. Manchester: Manchester University Press.

McCartin, J. (2013) *Collision Course: Ronald Reagan, the Air Traffic Controllers, and the Strike that Changed America*. New York: Oxford University Press.

McCloskey, R. G. (1951) *American Conservatism in the Age of Enterprise*. Cambridge, MA: Harvard University Press.

McGirr, L. (2001) *Suburban Warriors: The Origins of the New American Right*. Princeton, NJ: Princeton University Press.

MacIntyre, A. (1985) *After Virtue*. London: Duckworth.

Maddison, A. (1995) *Monitoring the World Economy, 1820–1992*. Paris: OECD.

Maistre, J. de (1820) *Du Pape*. Antwerp.

Maistre, J. de (1862) *Les Soirées de Saint-Pétersbourg, ou, Entretiens sur le Gouvernement Temporel de la Providence*. Lyon: J. B. Pelagaud.

Maistre, J. de (1884) *Œuvres Complètes*. 14 vols. Lyon: Vite.

Maistre, J. de (1980) *Considérations sur la France*. Paris: Garnier.

Maistre, J. de (1998) *An Examination of the Philosophy of Bacon wherein Different Questions of Rational Philosophy Are Treated*. ed. and trans. R. A. Lebrun. Montreal: McGill-Queens University Press.

Mallet du Pan (1793) *Considérations sur la Nature de la Révolution de France: Et sur les Causes qui en Prolongent la Durée*. Brussels: Chez E. Flon.

Mallock, W. H. (1884) 'Conservatism and Socialism', *National Review*, 2, pp. 696–702.

Mallock, W. H. (1893) *Labour and Popular Welfare*. London: Adam and Charles Black.

Mallock, W. H. (1898) *Aristocracy and Evolution*. London: Adam and Charles Black.

Mallock, W. H. (1908) *A Critical Examination of Socialism*. London: John Murray.

Mannheim, K. (1986) *Conservatism: A Contribution to the Sociology of Knowledge*, ed. D. Kettler, V. Meja and N. Stehr, trans. D. Kettler and V. Meja. London: Routledge.

Maritain, J. (1950a) *Christianity and Democracy*. New York: Scribner.

Maritain, J. (1950b) 'The Concept of Sovereignty', *American Political Science Review*, 44(2), pp. 343–57.

Maritain, J. (1958) *Réflexions sur l'Amérique*. Paris: Arthème Fayard.

Marwick, A. (2011) *The Sixties*. London: Bloomsbury.

Marx, K. (1977) *Selected Writings*, ed. and trans. D. McLellan. Oxford: Oxford University Press.

Marx, K. and Engels, F. (1965) *The German Ideology*, trans. S. Ryazanskaya. London: Lawrence and Wishart.

Mead, L. M. (1986) *Beyond Entitlement: The Social Obligations of Citizenship*. New York: Simon and Schuster.

Meadowcroft, J. (1995) *Conceptualizing the State: Innovation and Dispute in British Political Thought, 1880–1914*. Oxford: Clarendon Press.

Micklethwait, J. and Wooldridge, A. (2004) *The Right Nation: Why America Is Different*. London: Allen Lane.

Midgette, A. (2016) 'Donald Trump, Taste, and the Cultural Elite', *Washington Post*, 11 November.

Mommsen, W. (2011) 'German Liberalism in the Nineteenth Century', in G. Stedman Jones and G. Claeys, eds., *The Cambridge History of Nineteenth-Century Political Thought*. Cambridge: Cambridge University Press, pp. 409–32.

Mommsen, W. and Mock, W. (eds.) (1981) *The Emergence of the Welfare State in Britain and Germany, 1850–1950*. London: Croom Helm.

Morris, C. (2019) 'Brexit: Did Boris Johnson Talk Turkey during Referendum Campaign?' *BBC News*. Available at: https://www.bbc.co.uk/news/uk-politics-46926119.

Morrow, J. (2011) 'Romanticism and Political Thought in the Early Nineteenth Century', in G. Stedman Jones and G. Claeys, eds., *The Cambridge History of Nineteenth-Century Political Thought*. Cambridge: Cambridge University Press, pp. 39–76.

Muller, J.-W. (2013a) *Contesting Democracy: Political Ideas in Twentieth-Century Europe*. New Haven, CT: Yale University Press.

Muller, J.-W. (2013b) 'The Paradoxes of Post-war Italian Political Thought', *History of European Ideas*, 39(1), pp. 79–102.

Muller, J.-W. (2016) *What Is Populism?* Philadelphia: University of Pennsylvania Press.

Murray, C. (2012) *Coming Apart: The State of White America, 1960–2010*. New York: Random House.

Neill, E. (2006) 'Political Ideologies: Liberalism, Conservatism, and Socialism', in S. Berger, ed., *A Companion to Nineteenth-Century Europe, 1789–1914*. Oxford: Blackwell, pp. 211–23.

Neill, E. (2010) *Michael Oakeshott*. New York: Bloomsbury.

Neill, E. (2013) 'The Impact of Positivism: Academic Political Thought in Britain, c. 1945–1970', *History of European Ideas*, 39(1), pp. 51–78.

Neill, E. (2015) 'Oakeshott, Modernity, and Cold War Liberalism', in T. Nardin, ed., *Michael Oakeshott's Cold War Liberalism*. New York: Palgrave Macmillan, pp. 39–63.

Neill, E. (2017) 'The Nature of Oakeshott's Conservatism', in N. O'Sullivan, ed., *The Place of Michael Oakeshott in Contemporary Western and Non-Western Thought*. Exeter: Imprint Academic, pp. 90–106.

Neill, E. (2019) 'Conservative Thinkers and the Post-war State', in L. Goldman, ed., *Welfare and Social Policy in Britain since 1870*. Oxford: Oxford University Press, pp. 162–77.

Neill, E. (2020) 'Intellectual Reactions to Thatcherism: Conceptions of Citizenship and Civil Society from 1990–2010', in A. Mullen, S. Farrall and D. Jeffery, eds., *Thatcherism in the 21st Century: The Social and Cultural Legacy*. Basingstoke: Palgrave Macmillan, pp. 35–53.

Niles, N. (1983) 'Two Discourses on Liberty', in C. S. Hyneman and D. S. Lutz, eds., *American Political Writings during the Founding Era, 1760–1805*. 2 vols. Indianapolis, IN: Liberty Fund.

Nisbet, R. (1986) *Conservatism*. Milton Keynes: Open University Press.

Norman, J. (2010) *The Big Society*. Buckingham: University of Buckingham Press.

Oakeshott, M. (1975) *On Human Conduct*. Oxford: Clarendon Press.

Oakeshott, M. (1976) 'On Misunderstanding *On Human Conduct*: A Reply to My Critics', *Political Theory*, 4(3), pp. 353–67.

Oakeshott, M. (1991) *Rationalism in Politics and Other Essays*, ed. T. Fuller. Indianapolis, IN: Liberty Fund.

O'Rourke, K. (2014) 'From Empire to Europe: Britain in the World Economy', in R. Floud, J. Humphries and P. Johnson, eds., *The Cambridge Economic History of Modern Britain*. 3 vols. Cambridge: Cambridge University Press, II, pp. 60–94.

O'Sullivan, N. (1976) *Conservatism*. London: J. M. Dent.

Pareto, V. (1916) *Trattato di Sociolgia Generale*. 3 vols. Florence: G. Barbera.

Parry, J. P. (1993) *The Rise and Fall of Liberal Government in Victorian Britain*. New Haven, CT: Yale University Press.

Peele, G. (1984) *Revival and Reaction: The Right in Contemporary America*. Oxford: Clarendon Press.

Pocock, J. G. A. (1982) 'The Political Economy of Burke's Analysis of the French Revolution', *Historical Journal*, 25(2), pp. 331–49.

Pocock, J. G. A. (1985) *Virtue, Commerce, and History*. Cambridge: Cambridge University Press.

Pole, J. R. (1981) 'Enlightenment and the Politics of American Nature', in R. Porter and M. Teich, eds., *The Enlightenment in National Context*. Cambridge: Cambridge University Press, pp. 192–214.

Pollard, S. (1985) 'Capital Exports 1870–1914: Harmful or Beneficial?', *Economic History Review*, 38(4), pp. 489–514.

Porter, R. and Teich, M. (eds.) (1981) *The Enlightenment in National Context*. Cambridge: Cambridge University Press.

Reilly, K. (2016) 'Here Are All the Times Donald Trump Insulted Mexico', *Time*, 31 August.

Rosanvallon, P. (1994) *La Monarchie Impossible: Les Chartes de 1814 et de 1830*. Paris: Fayard.

Rousseau, J.-J. (1923) *The Social Contract and Discourses*, trans. G. D. H. Cole. London: J. M. Dent and Sons.

Ruskin, J. (1903–12) *The Works of John Ruskin*, ed. E. T. Cook and A. Wedderburn. 39 vols. London: George Allen.

Samuelson, R. (2003) 'John Adams and the Republic of Laws', in B.-P. Frost and J. Sikkenga, eds., *History of American Political Thought*. Lanham, MD: Lexington Books, pp. 114–31.

Schofield, C. (2012) '"A Nation or No Nation?" Enoch Powell and Thatcherism', in B. Jackson and R. Saunders, eds., *Making Thatcher's Britain*. Cambridge: Cambridge University Press, pp. 95–110.

Scott, M. (2015) *Chateaubriand: The Paradox of Change*. Bern: Peter Lang.

Scott-Smith, G. (2002) 'The Congress for Cultural Freedom, the End of Ideology and the 1955 Milan Conference: "Defining the Parameters of Discourse"', *Journal of Contemporary History*, 37(3), pp. 437–55.

Scruton, R. (1978) 'The Politics of Culture', in M. Cowling, ed., *Conservative Essays*. London: Cassell, pp. 101–16.

Scruton, R. (2001) *The Meaning of Conservatism*. Basingstoke: Palgrave Macmillan.

Seager, F. H. (1969) *The Boulanger Affair*. Ithaca, NY: Cornell University Press.

Singer, E. (1998) *20th Century Revolutions in Technology*. Commack, NY: Nova Science Publisher.

Southey, R. (1829) *Sir Thomas More: or Colloquies on the Progress and Prospects of Society*. 2 vols. London: John Murray.

Southey, R. (1832) *Essays, Moral and Political*. 2 vols. London: John Murray.

Spencer, H. (1876–96) *The Principles of Sociology*. 3 vols. London: Williams and Norgate.

Spencer, H. (1994) 'The Man versus the State', in H. Spencer, *Political Writings*, ed. J. Offer. Cambridge: Cambridge University Press, pp. 61–175.

Sperber, J. (2005) *The European Revolutions, 1848–51*. Cambridge: Cambridge University Press.

Sternhall, Z. (2001) 'Fascism: Reflections on the Fate of Ideas in Twentieth-Century History', in M. Freeden, ed., *Reassessing Ideologies: The Durability of Dissent*. London: Routledge, pp. 92–115.

Strauss, L. (1953) *Natural Right and History*. Chicago: University of Chicago Press.

Strauss, L. (1964) *The City and Man*. New York: Rand McNally.

Strauss, L. (1968) *Liberalism Ancient and Modern*. Ithaca, NY: Cornell University Press.

Strauss, L. (1975) *Political Philosophy: Six Essays*, ed. H. Gilden. Indianapolis, IN: Pegasus Books.

Sumner, W. G. (1963) *Social Darwinism: Selected Essays*, ed. S. Persons. Englewood Cliffs, NJ: Prentice-Hall.

Susskind, J. (2011) *Karl Marx and British Intellectuals in the 1930s*. Oxford: Davenant Press.

Taggart, P. (2004) 'Populism and Representative Politics in Contemporary Europe', *Journal of Political Ideologies*, 9(3), pp. 269–88.

Vincent, A. (2010) *Modern Political Ideologies*. Oxford: Wiley-Blackwell.

Wardley, P. (2011) 'The Economy', in G. Martel, ed., *A Companion to Europe, 1900–1945*. Oxford: Blackwell, pp. 98–116.

Webb, B. and Webb, S. (1897) *Industrial Democracy*. 2 vols. London: Longmans, Green and Co.

Weiss, J. (1977) *Conservatism in Europe, 1770–1945: Traditionalism, Reaction, and Counter-revolution*. London: Thames and Hudson.

Weldon, T. D. (1953) *The Vocabulary of Politics*. Harmondsworth: Penguin.

Westfall, R. S. (1980) *Never at Rest: A Biography of Isaac Newton*. Cambridge: Cambridge University Press.

Willetts, D. (1997) 'Civic Conservatism', in J. Gray and D. Willetts, *Is Conservatism Dead?* London: Profile Books, pp. 69–141.

Williamson, P. (2003) 'The Doctrinal Politics of Stanley Baldwin', in M. Bentley, ed., *Public and Private Doctrine*. Cambridge: Cambridge University Press, pp. 181–208.

Withnall, A. (2016) 'EU Referendum: Nigel Farage's 4am Victory Speech – the Text in Full', *The Independent*, 24 June.

Wood, G. S. (1993) *The Radicalism of the American Revolution*. New York: Vintage.

Worsthorne, P. (1978) 'Too Much Freedom', in M. Cowling, ed., *Conservative Essays*. London: Cassell, pp. 141–54.

Wright, A. (2013) *British Politics: A Very Short Introduction*. Oxford: Oxford University Press.

Young, J. P. (2011) 'American Political Thought from Jeffersonian Republicanism to Progressivism', in G. Stedman Jones and G. Claeys, eds., *The Cambridge History of Nineteenth-Century Political Thought*. Cambridge: Cambridge University Press, pp. 374–408.

Young, J. P. (2018) *Reconsidering American Liberalism: The Troubled Odyssey of the Liberal Idea*. London: Routledge.

Index